# THE BEHAVIOR OF PENGUINS

SUNY Series in Animal Behavior
Jerram L. Brown, Editor

# THE BEHAVIOR OF PENGUINS
## ADAPTED TO ICE AND TROPICS

Dietland Müller-Schwarze

STATE UNIVERSITY OF NEW YORK PRESS
Albany

Published by
State University of New York Press, Albany
© 1984 State University of New York
All rights reserved
Printed in the United States of America

For information, address State University of New York
Press, State University Plaza, Albany, N.Y., 12246

Library of Congress Cataloging in Publication Data

Müller-Schwarze, Dietland.
   The behavior of penguins.

   (SUNY series in animal behavior)
   Bibliography: p.
   1. Penguins—Behavior. I. Title. II. Series.
QL696.S473M82   1984        598.4'41        83-18020
ISBN 0-87395-866-7
ISBN 0-87395-867-5 (pbk.)


10   9   8   7   6   5   4   3   2   1

# CONTENTS ————————————————

# PART II  THE PENGUIN SPECIES

# LIST OF MAPS _____

viii

# PREFACE

Clouds are gathering over the "bottom of the world." The 1982 Falkland Islands war and the 1983 oil spill off South Africa are merely harbingers of more turmoil to come. Whalers and sealers have depleted stocks in the past. As more countries join the club of interested nations, satisfactory agreements are increasingly difficult to reach. Minerals, oil, gas, even fresh water are keenly eyed as resources. For now, the Antarctic Treaty, which will expire in 1991, protects wildlife, facilitates international cooperation in research, holds territorial claims in abeyance, and prohibits military exercises and nuclear disposal, but leaves open the question of commercial exploitation of the Antarctic. Given an accelerating scramble for resources, new treaty negotiations will be more complex and frustrating, especially since more than the original twelve signatory countries are now involved.

The international agreements, rather than weakened, should be expanded, elaborated, and made permanent to create a formal international Antarctic Wildlife Range which may or may not be opened periodically to resource exploitation in part or as a whole, and under carefully specified conditions. Since this is a new concept, I deliberately avoid designations such as Park, Sanctuary, or Wildlife Management Area.

Krill fishing and tourist cruises are now part of the Antarctic scene, exerting opposing pressures on the ecosystem. The former threatens to deprive penguins and other polar animals of their food base, while the tourists demand to view and photograph intact wildlife in a pristine environment. More airstrips, a hotel, and whole families have recently been added to the traditional community of scientific stations.

In the midst of all this change the original inhabitants, penguins, other seabirds, seals and whales continue their age-old cycles of breeding, migration, and predation. Will there be an equilibrium between the rapid change brought by man to this region and the tenacity and adaptability of the birds and mammals who call it home? Should we actively seek such an equilibrium through management? If so, do we have the necessary knowledge base?

Wildlife management is based on intricate knowledge of the behavior and ecology of the organisms in question. It is in this spirit that this book has been written. If we know in great detail, and consider reproductive behavior and capacity, food and habitat requirements, migrations, predation effects, and other biodata we will be able to minimize adverse impact on penguins and other members of the ecosystem. Kooyman (*Weddell Seal: Consummate Diver*, Cambridge Univ. Press, 1981) has pointed out that Antarctic seals and birds are the only great populations of large animals left whose population and distribution limits are set by rules of nature, not by man.

Penguins are affected by man in various ways. Visitors disturb breeding colonies, indiscriminate krill fishing depletes their food base, they are defenseless against introduced predators (dogs) and diseases, not to mention the obvious dangers of habitat destruction and the pollution of water, air, and land. The "harvesting" of penguins was once an officially approved enterprise but was later outlawed. It has been planned again for South America as recently as 1982. Adélie penguins, skuas and petrels have been found to contain levels of chlorinated hydrocarbon pesticides that already resemble those found in animals of northern latitudes (Riseborough and Carmignani 1972), while emperor penguin carcasses left by Edward Wilson in 1911 during the "Worst Journey of the World" did not contain any (Sladen et al. 1966).

Why are penguins worth protecting? There are at least four reasons. First, having colonized the ice-bound shores of the southernmost continent as well as tropical islands, penguins offer priceless insights into adaptive radiation and evolution. To damage or destroy an ecosystem before we have understood it is inexcusable, considering our current scientific capabilities. Second, there is a growing number of travelers who appreciate penguins in their environment for their aesthetic value. Thus the argument that hardly anybody ever sees these remote animals no longer holds. The willingness to pay for the privilege to view wildlife in out-of-the-way places provides the third incentive for conservation. Tourism is a non-consumptive use of wildlife, providing increasing profits to a growing industry. The fourth, in my opinion, is the most compelling reason for restraint: we cannot reconstitute a species once it has become extinct. We may be able to renovate certain habitats by replanting forests, for instance—but we are unable to fashion a king penguin after its extermination as a species. It is the irreversibility of events that counts here. A world with some natural marvels left is preferable to one where every square meter is used to support an immense human population, or, worse, one in which a large part of food production is devoted to pets in affluent countries.

Penguins are but a special case of the general question: "Why is it worth saving any species or ecosystem?" There is no general answer. Rather than being based on rational, irrefutable reasons, our attitude toward conservation is rooted in our value systems, which vary from culture to culture and between individuals within a culture. Scientists think of preserving genetic, and hence biochemical diversity, hunters and trappers protect out of self-interest to maintain a harvestable population. Native North Americans would cite respect for brother creatures, and many people in industrialized countries sympathize with rare, defenseless, or aesthetically appealing animals.

Taking these attitudes into account, management and conservation efforts can be based on a cost/benefit ratio. The destructive effects on ecosystems by certain types of resource exploitation can be measured not only by disturbed or disappearing populations or habitat, but particularly by the attitudinal resistance it creates. With increasing decimation more and more people become concerned and rally to the defense of the threatened entity. A point will be reached at which this nonmaterial cost exceeds the material benefit from the resource. A worldwide public outcry outweighs the profits for perhaps only one company, or even food obtained for a certain number of people. Thus in addition to the traditional environmental impact statements we have to consider the potential mental impact on offended parties. This impact will intensify with increased pressure on the resource. It was exactly such public outcry that stopped the rendering for oil of king and royal penguins on Macquarie Island early in this century. In our days, a worldwide protest prevented the 1982 plans to commercially exploit penguins in Patagonia. Here, in addition to appeals to act in a "civilized" fashion, weight was carried by the argument that continued non-consumptive viewing of penguins by tourists will prove more lucrative in the long run than short-sighted depletion and habitat destruction.

This review covers the literature through 1982. It was my intent to highlight pertinent studies, and it is not meant to be exhaustive. It is hoped the book will be useful to a broad audience, including, but not limited to, ornithological and behavioral researchers, graduate and undergraduate students, as well as the "educated non-specialist".

Figs. 7, 19, 20, 32, 39, 40, 43, 50, 51, and 52, are by DMS and are reprinted from a German-language book entitled "Pinguine" with permission of Ziemsen Verlag, Wittenberg Lutherstadt, Germany.

My thanks go to the National Science Foundation for making possible various research trips to the Antarctic, and especially to Dr. George A. Llano for his understanding and encouragement, my wife Christine for assistance and companionship in the field, Captain Pieter Lennie of the R/V *Hero* for logistics support, and Dr. Frank S. Todd for help and advice. Society Expeditions enabled me to collect data on remote islands, and I am especially grateful to Werner Zehnder and Captain Heinz Aye. I thank Ms. Ruth Piatoff for typing the manuscript.

Syracuse, November 1983                    Dietland Müller-Schwarze

# Part I.

## _____PENGUINS IN GENERAL

Penguins are familiar to everyone, and yet few people have had the opportunity to observe them in their natural habitat in remote regions.

This is at the same time an introduction into penguin behavior and a review of recent research. The author is familiar with 13 species of penguins in their natural habitat on the various southern continents and islands.

# Chapter 1

## HISTORY _____

The first penguins were discovered in 1520 during Magellan's circumnavigation. Pigafetta, the historian of the expedition, called them "strange geese" (Murphy 1959).

In 1758 Linné mentioned 2 penguin species in his *Systema Naturae:* the black-footed penguin of South Africa ("Diomedea demersa"; today *Spheniscus demersus*), and the rockhopper penguin of South America ("Phaethon demersus"; today: *Eudyptes crestatus*). Pennant described the king penguin (*Aptenodytes patagonica*) in 1768, and Sonnerat the Magellan penguin (*Spheniscus magellanicus*) and gentoo penguin (*Pygoscelis papua*). Forster, naturalist on Captain Cook's circumnavigation, in 1781 listed 9 penguin species. Of these, 4 were new ones.

The next valid species, the macaroni penguin, *Eudyptes chrysolophus*, was described by Brandt in 1837. In 1841 Hombron and Jacquinot added 2 more species: Adélie penguin (*Pygoscelis adeliae*) and yellow-eyed penguin (*Megadyptes antipodes*). Gray (1844) described *Eudyptes pachyrhynchus*, the Fjordland penguin from New Zealand waters. The emperor penguin was described in 1844, after the expedition of Sir James Clark Ross.

Coves (1872) lists 13 species; and Schlegel's taxonomy of 1876 is still used today in principle.

The Galapagos penguin (*Spheniscus mendiculus*) was added in 1871, in 1874 the white-flippered penguin (*Eudyptula albosignata*), and in 1876 the royal penguin (*Eudyptes schlegeli*) from Macquarie Island. In 1953 the Snares Island penguin (*Eudyptes robustus*) was declared an independent species.

Today we distinguish 18 (Murphy 1959; Stonehouse 1968) or 17 (Alexander and Niethammer 1959) species of penguins.

# Chapter 2

# PENGUINS IN GENERAL _____

## FORM

Penguins are a bird group easy to define; there are no transitions to other bird forms. The shortest description is "flightless seabird." The wings have evolved into flippers, which lack the long primaries and secondaries, and have instead a uniform cover of short, stiff, scale-like feathers.

Body shape and life habits are a consequence of breeding on islands and coasts that are generally inaccessible to land predators. Underwater flight and upright posture on land have favored strong, flat flippers, and posteriorly attached legs, respectively.

"Pinguis" means "fat" in Latin. The original *Pinguinus* was the Great Auk of the northern hemisphere, of which the last specimen was killed in Iceland in 1847. Today, the term "penguin" survives for similar, but not directly related flightless seabirds of the southern hemisphere.

Penguins share many features with other seabirds, such as salt glands, colonial breeding and its consequences, such as peculiarities of territorial fighting, threat and courtship behaviors, and individual recognition. Foraging breeders and non-breeders at sea are highly social; single penguins on the high seas are the exception.

5

## LOCOMOTION

On land, penguins walk upright, since the legs are attached more posteriorly than in other birds. The large species, in particular, such as the heavy emperor and king penguins, walk slowly and awkwardly. Among the small species, the rockhopper jumps from boulder to boulder. On steep ice slopes emperor and Adélie penguins use their beaks like ice picks. On level or slightly sloping snow, the Antarctic species, including the emperor penguin, slide on their bellies, being propelled by their legs, and steadied by their flippers ("tobogganing").

Water being the medium for foraging, migration and anti-predator behavior, it is not surprising that there are several efficient styles of swimming: "underwater flight" with often rapid turns during feeding or predator avoidance, "porpoising" (leaping out of the water at regular intervals) for long-distance swimming, feeding swimming with only the back above water, and "duck-style" with head and tail erect. The latter posture is assumed when penguins have reached just off-shore and orient themselves before swimming or leaping on to the land.

## THE PENGUIN SPECIES

Currently we distinguish 18 species of penguins. If one considers the 3 subspecies each of gentoo and little penguin, we are dealing with 22 different forms. This, however, may change in the future, as the taxonomy of penguins, especially the crested penguins, is still in flux. For instance, Jouventin (1982) has proposed to recognize 2 separate species of rockhoppers. The penguin species are listed below.

Table 1.  The 18 Penguin Species and Their Scientific Names

| | |
|---|---|
| 1. *Aptenodytes forsteri* | Emperor penguin |
| 2. *Aptenodytes patagonica* | King penguin |
| 3. *Pygoscelis papua* | Gentoo penguin |
| *P. p. ellsworthi* | |
| *P. p. papua* | |
| *P. p. taeniata* | |
| 4. *Pygoscelis adeliae* | Adélie penguin |
| 5. *Pygoscelis antarctica* | Chinstrap penguin |

Table 1.  The 18 Penguin Species and Their Scientific Names

| | |
|---|---|
| 6. *Spheniscus humboldti* | Peruvian penguin |
| 7. *Spheniscus magellanicus* | Magellanic penguin |
| 8. *Spheniscus demersus* | Black-footed penguin |
| 9. *Spheniscus mendiculus* | Galapagos penguin |
| 10. *Eudyptes chrysolophus* | Macaroni penguin |
| 11. *Eudyptes crestatus* | Rockhopper penguin |
| 12. *Eudyptes schlegeli* | Royal penguin |
| 13. *Eudyptes pachyrhynchus* | Fjordland penguin |
| 14. *Eudyptes robustus* | Snares-Island penguin |
| 15. *Eudyptes sclateri* | Erect crested penguin |
| 16. *Eudyptula minor* | Little blue penguin |
| *E. m. minor*<br>*E. m. novaehollandiae*<br>*E. m. iredalei*<br>17. *Eudyptula albosignata* | White-flippered penguin |
| 18. *Megadyptes antipodes* | Yellow-eyed penguin |

## PENGUINS BY GROUPS

Penguins range in body weight from 30 kg (or more in captivity) for the emperor penguin to slightly over 1 kg (little blue penguin).

The 2 largest species, emperor and king penguin, are similar in appearance and behavior and form the genus *Aptenodytes* (Gk. "flightless diver"). The emperor penguin, *A. forsteri*, (after the zoologist Reinhold Forster who accompanied Cook on his circumnavigation) is not only the largest penguin, but also holds several other biological records. He is the only bird that does not need to visit solid land for his entire lifetime, dives up to 60 m deep and can fast for over 4 months.

The king penguin (*A. patagonica*) is similar to the emperor penguin, but smaller. It weighs only about 16 kg and is a somewhat familiar bird to zoo visitors. The diagnostic plumage features of the king are the bright orange on the neck, and the corners of the dark-grey back plumage that reach each other almost at the front of the throat. The king penguin is subantarctic, while the emperor breeds at the coasts of the Antarctic continent and is distributed circumpolarly.

The genus *Pygoscelis* or long-tailed penguins are of medium size (4.5– 6.5 kg). It comprises three species: the Adélie penguin, *Pygoscelis adeliae* (named after Adélie Land, which, in turn, Durmont d'Urville had named after his wife), the gentoo penguin, *P. papua* (named in the 18th century after an erroneous "collection site" in New Guinea), and the chinstrap penguin, *P. antarctica*.

The most northerly pygoscelid species is the gentoo. It occurs on subantarctic islands from the Falkland Islands in the west to Macquarie Island in the east, and penetrates into the Antarctic Peninsula, where the southernmost known colony is located on Petermann Island. The chinstrap is intermediate in its distribution: it breeds on subantarctic and Antarctic islands in the American-Atlantic quadrant. The Adélie, finally, is typical for the Antarctic continent. Together with the emperor penguin, it is one of the two most southern penguin species and is circumpolarly distributed. The three species of pygoscelids are easily distinguished by their head markings. The gentoo has a white "bonnet" across the top of the head, and a bright red bill. The chinstrap has a black stripe across the chin, which, together with the black top of the head, gives the bird the appearance of wearing a helmet. The Adélie has a black head and chin, and white eye rings which are most prominent during the breeding season.

The genus *Spheniscus* (Gr. "wedge shaped") is well-known to the zoo visitor in the form of the once common Humboldt (or Peruvian) penguin, *S. humboldti*. It lives along the coasts of Peru and Chile. Further to the south and on the east shores of southern South America, lives the Magellanic penguin, *S. magellanicus*. Its range overlaps with that of *S. humboldti* in central Chile. It has 2 black bands across the neck, while the Peruvian penguin has only 1. The third South American species is the Galapagos penguin, *S. mendiculus* (Lat. "little beggar"). Finally, the black-footed penguin, *S. demersus* (Lat. "dived under") of the west and south coast of South Africa resembles superficially the Peruvian penguin in its head markings. Because of its voice it is also called "jackass penguin", a term sometimes applied to all 4 species.

The crested penguins, genus *Eudyptes* (Gk. "good diver") possess on their heads more or less elongated yellow plumes. The macaroni penguin, *E. chrysolophus* (Gk. "golden feather tuft") breeds on subantarctic islands from the southern tip of South America to the middle of the Indian Ocean (75° E). The closely related royal penguin, *E. schlegeli*, takes its place in the Southern Ocean south of Australia and New Zealand, and is possibly the same species. Its cheeks and throat are white and it breeds in large aggregations on Macquarie Island. The rockhopper penguin, *E. crestatus* (Lat. "tufted" or "crested"), distributed over the subantarctic belt, breeds from Tierra del Fuego eastward to the islands south of New Zealand. The Fjordland penguin, *E. pachyrhynchus* (Gr. "thick bill") is confined to the fjords in southwest New Zealand, while the erect-crested penguin, *E. sclateri*, breeds on the Antipodes, Bounty and Campbell Islands in the New Zealand sector. Finally, the Snares Island penguin, *E. robustus*, from the islands of the same name (south of New Zealand) is considered a species distinct from the Fjordland penguin. The two smallest penguin species comprise the genus *Eudyptula*: *E. minor*, the little blue penguin, occurs in South Australia and New Zealand, while the white-flippered penguin *E. albosignata*, is restricted to the Banks Peninsula on the east coast of the South Island of New Zealand. The eighteenth and last species is the yellow-eyed penguin, *Megadyptes antipodes* (Gk. "large diver from the Antipodes"), found in southern New Zealand and on islands to the south.

# Chapter 3

# ZOOGEOGRAPHIC REGIONS AND THEIR CHARACTERISTIC PENGUINS_____

Penguins have radiated from the southern temperate zone mostly south to the subantarctic and Antarctic zones, but also north to the tropics. In addition to this latitudinal stratification, penguins are longitudinally divided into New Zealand/Australian, South American, and African forms. In the subantarctic some forms are also restricted to certain quadrants.

Starting from the south, we distinguish two circumpolar zones: the Antarctic and the subantarctic, to the south and north of the Antarctic convergence, respectively. The Antarctic zone can be divided into the continental Antarctic which encompasses the Antarctic continent with the exception of the Antarctic Peninsula. This peninsula and the outlying island chains form the maritime Antarctic.

The subantarctic zone consists of 3 subzones: The transition subzone at the Antarctic Convergence, the cold subantarctic subzone immediately to the north, and the temperate subantarctic subzone further north. The 10° C Isotherme at 40–45° south latitude separates the latter two subzones. The northern limit of the temperate subantarctic subzone is the subtropical convergence. The better known subantarctic islands belong to the transition subzone. These are South Georgia, Kerguelen, Heard and Macquarie Islands. Zoogeographically, the subantarctic region can be divided into the Atlantic, Kerguelen, and New Zealand provinces.

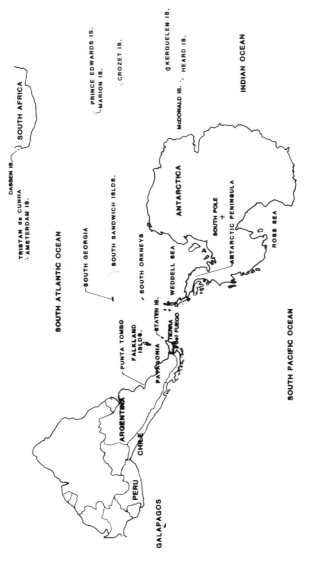

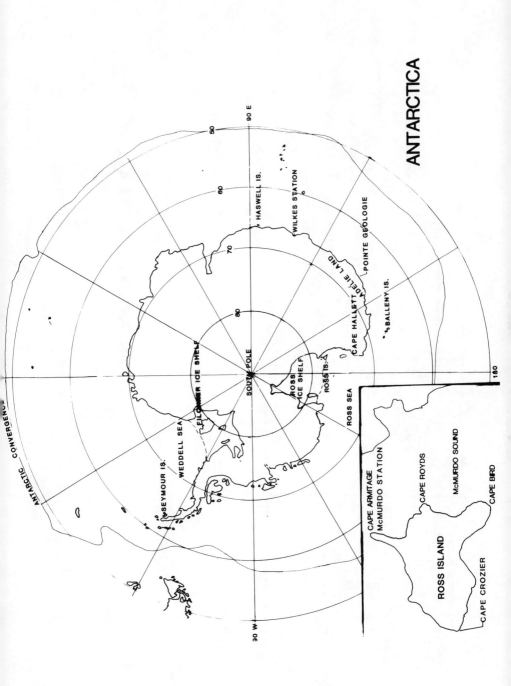

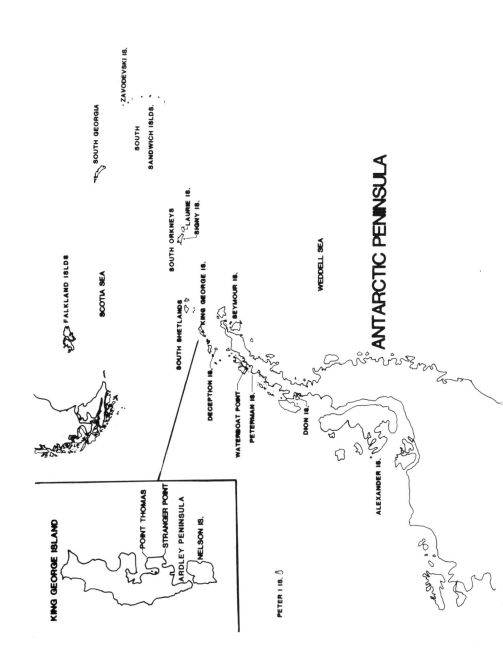

Figure 1.   The 3 species of pygoscelid penguins breeding side by side. Adélie on upper left, Chinstrap on lower left, Gentoo on lower right. Ardley Peninsula, King George Island.

## ANTARCTIC PENGUINS

*Continental Antarctic Penguins.*
The emperor and Adélie penguins are the species typical for the Antarctic continent and the islands at its fringe. Their breeding habitats differ: the emperor uses continuous fast-ice for its colonies (and is the only bird that does so), while the Adélie breeds on ice-free coastal rock slopes. Non-breeding birds of both species may share the same ice floe. Both species are distributed circumpolarly.

*Maritime Antarctic Penguins.*
The chinstrap penguin is characteristic for the maritime subzone. It is particularly common on the South Shetland and South Orkney islands. The gentoo penguin shares the maritime subzone, but reaches its southern limit there. It extends northward into the cold subantarctic subzone. The Adélie on the other hand, reaches its northern limit in the maritime subzone. Thus, all 3 pygoscelid penguins occur in the maritime subzone, and sometimes share the same rookery, as at Ardley Peninsula, Stranger Point (Fig. 1), and Point Thomas, all on King George Island in the South Shetlands, and in the Joubin Islands.

## SUBANTARCTIC PENGUINS

The *Transition Zone* is the home of the king penguin, which also occurs in the cold subantarctic subzone. Chinstrap and gentoo live here, as do rockhopper and macaroni penguins. The royal penguin on Macquarie Island is considered by some merely a subspecies of the Macaroni penguin.

In the *cold subantarctic subzone* occur king, chinstrap, rockhopper and macaroni penguins.

In the *temperate subantarctic subzone* belong the South American penguins (Magellan, and, to a certain extent, Humboldt) and those of the New Zealand area (yellow-eyed, little blue, white-flippered, Fjordland, Snares-Island, and erect-crested penguins).

## TEMPERATE ZONE AND TROPICAL PENGUINS

*Temperate zone* Here we find the blackfooted (or jackass) penguin of South Africa, and in the tropics the Galapagos penguin and the Humboldt penguin of the Chilean and Peruvian coasts.

# Chapter 4

# PENGUINS AS
# SOCIAL BIRDS _____

Some penguin rookeries number millions of birds, although this is excep-
tional. There are at least 2 rookeries of Magellanic penguins in Argentina
that number about 1 million birds: Punta Tombo, and Camarones to the
south. Adélie penguins number about 5 million on Laurie Island in the
South Orkneys, and a large chinstrap rookery at Zavodevski Island in the
South Sandwich group has been estimated to number 10 million birds.
On Beauchene Island in the Falklands there are 5–6 million rockhoppers
(Strange 1965) and "millions" of the same species in Franklin Bay, Staten
Island, off the tip of Tierra del Fuego (Boswall and MacIver 1975).

Why are penguins so highly social during the breeding season, on
migration and in their winter quarters? They share this trait with other
colonially breeding seabirds, and it is highly adaptive. Physical features of
the environment such as limited space suitable for breeding, or a highly
localized food supply may force seabirds to breed closely together.

But even if alternatives are available, penguins tend to build up one
rookery to immense numbers, and rarely colonize new areas. One such
case occurred in McMurdo Sound where 3 pairs of emperor penguins
started breeding, but disappeared later (G. Llano pers. comm.). Social
factors are responsible for this: the proximate reason for the large aggregations of penguins is that mature penguins return to their natal rookery
for breeding (philopatry). But why? The ultimate reasons are increased

safety from aquatic and aerial predators, mutual stimulation leading to synchronized breeding, and the opportunity to learn from others about food locations (the "information center" hypothesis). Living in groups provides an anti-predator advantage at all seasons, hence penguins breed, travel, forage, migrate and winter over in groups. Synchronization of breeding not only permits communal chick defense and simultaneous migration but protects the young from excessive predation: large numbers of eggs at the same time or same-age chicks "swamp" the predator, and are available to him only for the shortest possible time.

The basic social unit is the family, consisting of both adults and typically 2 young, with the nest as territory and activity center. Feeding and defense of the young against other penguins are the activities taking place at the nest. At the level of the breeding group (or colony) anti-skua defense is a social activity, and mutual stimulation, notably by vocalizations, leads to synchronized breeding. Communal crèche protection is another function of the breeding group. Since offspring tend to settle down close to their natal nests, the breeding group members are possibly more closely related than they are with penguins of other colonies. This would mean that relatives help each other with guarding and defending the young, and intraspecific competition may take place at the level of the colony.

# Chapter 5

# PENGUINS AS DIVING BIRDS_____

Penguins are the only avian order of which all species are flightless and specialized for diving. It is not surprising that their extraordinary adaptations to the oceanic life have attracted the attention of physiologists for the study of the diving behavior and the associated physiological processes. This account draws heavily on the results reported by Kooyman and his co-workers.

The diving behavior and diving depth of penguins depend on the depth of their prey which may vary with the seasons and with the time of day. The main diet of penguins encompasses crustaceans, fish, and cephalopods. Most food organisms of the penguins live in the upper water layers so that penguins in general do not have to dive deep or for a long duration. Emperor penguins hold the record; they can dive for up to 18 minutes. But most penguins and other diving birds are typically submerged for 1 minute or less. Gentoo penguins dive for up to two minutes. In laboratory experiments, gentoo and Adélie penguins tolerated forced submersion for maximally 7 minutes (Kooyman 1975). The depth of diving in emperor penguins varies from 45 to 265 meters (Kooyman et al 1971), and king penguins sometimes surpass 240 m (Kooyman et al. 1982).

A diving bird has to overcome 3 main difficulties: lack of oxygen during the dive, compression effects due to the high hydrostatic pressure, and thermoregulation in the water. Generally speaking, diving birds minimize the probability of harmful effects by making shallow dives of short duration. Birds carry their oxygen stores in the blood hemoglobin, the myoglobin of the muscles, and in the air of the lungs and air sacs. Penguins and other diving birds have more blood than non-diving birds, and there is a tendency for their blood to have a higher oxygen capacity. But all birds investigated thus far have less blood in relation to their body size than, for example, the Weddell seal (*Leptonychotes weddelli*) which has been thoroughly investigated by Kooyman (1981).

Waterbirds usually have more myoglobin than land birds. Despite this, the oxygen reserve in the myoglobin is first exhausted during the dive, and the muscles continue to obtain energy via the less efficient anaerobic metabolism. Myoglobin has a greater oxygen affinity than hemoglobin. Therefore, the muscles have to be shut off from the other oxygen stores of the body. They would deprive other vital organs, such as the brain, of oxygen.

Compared to seals, the proportion of oxygen that penguins store in lungs and air sacs is very high. This air contains 50% of the total oxygen. Of the remainder, fifteen percent is bound to myoglobin, and 30–35% is in the blood. A 5 kg penguin has an estimated oxygen reserve of about 250 ml. This would last for about 2.5 minutes at resting metabolism. Taking into account the various oxygen-saving mechanisms during diving, the oxygen in the body may last up to 6 minutes.

During the dive Adélie and gentoo penguins reduce their heart rate from 80–100 to 20 (Kooyman 1975), and the muscles, such as the gastrocnemius and pectoralis muscles, obtain less blood, while the heart receives a maximum. The lactic acid concentration in the blood increases gradually during the dive, and dramatically after the dive. This indicates anaerobic processes in the muscles which are supplied with little blood during the dive, but generously suffused after emerging. As is to be expected, the oxygen content of the blood drops rapidly during the dive, and the carbon dioxide level increases correspondingly. Compared to seals, penguins are not very economical with their oxygen stores.

Diving birds and mammals are less sensitive to carbon dioxide than land animals. The reason for this is most likely the greater buffering ability of the blood of penguins and other diving vertebrates.

The effects on the penguin body of the raised hydrostatic pressure are less well investigated. According to Kooyman emperor penguins dive up to 265 m deep. At this depth gas-filled body cavities will be compressed to one twenty-sixth of their volume at sea-level. In penguins the gas volume in relation to body size is so large that the nitrogen content of the blood may reach more dangerous levels than in seals (danger of "the bends"). Their blood probably does not take up much nitrogen because penguins usually dive not very deep and not for very long.

The thermoregulation under water in penguins is little understood.

Based on observations on land one assumes that the feathers are responsible for 80% of the thermal insulation, and the blubber for the rest. The insulating effect of the plumage is due to air bubbles trapped in the feathers. These bubbles are compressed during the dive and can get lost after prolonged diving so that the feathers have to be re-arranged by "preening."

Penguins have to strike a compromise between the requirements for aquatic and terrestrial locomotion. Because of their peculiar anatomy, locomotion on land costs penguins more energy than other birds, or quadrupeds, such as mammals. A 5 kg Adélie penguin needs about 7.5 kilojoule for waddling 1 km (Pinshow et al. 1977). The maximum waddling speed of emperor penguins is 2.8 km/hr and that of Adélie penguins 3.9 km/hr (Pinshow et al. 1977).

# Chapter 6

# THE PHYLOGENY OF PENGUINS

Penguin evolution has intrigued biologists ever since it was suggested by Menzbier in 1887 (Simpson 1946) that their flightlessness may represent a second, independent link to the reptiles in parallel evolution to other birds.

The question of the phylogeny of penguins led to "The Worst Journey in the World" (Cherry-Garrard 1922), a sledge trek to Cape Crozier, one of the most heroic undertakings of all time. During Robert Falcon Scott's tragic second Antarctic expedition (1910-13), E. A. Wilson and two companions man-hauled two sleds for 5 weeks during the polar night to obtain incubated emperor penguin eggs for embryological studies. Temperatures dropped to −60° C, and storm winds reached 200 km/h. The men, 2 of whom perished later with Scott on the way back from the South Pole, collected eggs, of which 3 finally reached the Museum of Natural History in London. But for many years nobody studied them (Cherry-Garrard 1922). "Wilson's Igloo," a shelter built above the emperor penguins during the "Worst Journey" rookery, can still be seen (Müller-Schwarze and Müller-Schwarze 1972).

Thomas Henry Huxley described the first fossil penguin in 1859 after bones found in New Zealand. Today we know 17 extinct genera, and 32 species (Simpson 1946, 1975). Fossil penguins have been found in Australia, New Zealand, Patagonia, Seymour Island (Antarctica), and South

Africa. The fossils from Australia, New Zealand, and Antarctica are from the late Eocene, those from South America early Miocene, and those from South Africa late Miocene.

Penguins are derived from flying birds. The transition from a flying bird to one that "flies under water,"air, is exemplified today in the diving petrels (Pelecanoididae). The closest surviving relatives of penguins are the petrels (Procellariiformes). The two groups have similar egg-white albumins and uropygial gland secretions.

The oldest penguin fossils are from the late Eocene, and the oldest known Procellariiform is an albatros from the middle Eocene (Simpson 1975). Therefore, the common origin of the 2 groups remains unknown. In fact, the oldest bird fossils in the southern hemisphere are probably of Eocene age, again too late to shed any light on the radiation of birds in general, and the origin of penguins in particular (Simpson 1975).

The extinct penguins were more diverse and larger in size than the recent forms. The extinction of the large penguins may have been related to competition by pinnipeds that rose in the Miocene, and by small Miocene cetaceans. Thus, with the pelagic niche for larger penguins taken over by those mammals, only the smaller forms survived (Simpson 1975).

# Chapter 7

## THE ROLE OF PENGUINS IN THE ECOSYSTEM_____

Penguins are carnivores and obtain all their energy from the ocean. They feed on crustaceans, fish and cephalopods, and are in turn the prey of large animals, such as leopard seals, sea lions, and killer whales.

Feeding strategies of sympatric penguin species are little known. On South Georgia gentoo penguins feed on fish and larger krill (*Euphausia superba*) while the macaroni penguin takes smaller krill of the same species. The macaroni penguin stays longer at sea, and forages at greater distances from land than the gentoo penguin, essentially outside the feeding range of the latter. The gentoo raises two young, while the macaroni penguin raises only one. Hence, the gentoo penguin has to return more often (every day) and cannot travel as far as the macaroni which feeds up to 50 km from shore at the edge of the island shelf, and stays at sea for 2 days during each feeding trip (Croxall and Prince 1980).

The most significant competitor for krill at South Georgia is the Antarctic fur seal, *Arctocephalus gazella*, of which there are about 370,000 at that island (Croxall and Prince 1980).

It has been suggested that the drastic decrease in the whale stock has made available vast amounts of krill for consumption by seabirds, among them penguins. A potential population increase by 300 million pygoscelid penguins has been predicted (Sladen 1964). But it is not clear that all this krill is available to penguins which, at least during the breeding period, are limited to feeding areas comparatively close to the coasts of Antarctica and the subantarctic islands.

Penguins influence their habitat not only by creating hills in their colonies from the continued accumulation of pebbles, but also by nutrient cycling: They deposit nitrogen and phosphorus on the land in the form of guano, which fills the gaps between the pebbles that are piled up in the course of repeated nestings on the same sites. In chinstrap colonies, 10 kg of biomass is accumulated per m$^2$ (or 2-16 grams per day).

Especially the subantarctic islands with their richer vegetation experience accumulation of nitrogen and phosphorus in or near penguin rookeries. On Macquarie Island, the total nitrogen content within 50 m and downwind from a colony of royal penguins was 8.69 g/m$^2$/yr. This compares with 1.57 and 2.72 g/m$^2$/yr, respectively, in other areas of Macquarie Island. The worldwide range is 0.07 - 2.37 g/m$^2$/yr (Jenkin 1975). Similarly, in South Georgia high nitrogen and phosphorus concentrations are found in coastal tussock grass (*Poa flabellata*) frequented by penguins and seals, and on slopes where excrements from terns or burrowing petrels seep into the ground (Smith and Waldon 1975). On Signy Island, sea spray returns nitrogen and phosphorus from the bird rookeries and seal wallows to the higher slopes (Collins et al. 1975).

# Chapter 8

# PENGUINS ARE
# SPECIAL BIRDS _____

A bird as specialized as a penguin is characterized by several drastic anatomical and physiological adaptations, and penguins that have colonized extreme polar habitat have further modified their body structure, physiology, feeding habits, social organization and timing of their activities.

Among the general adaptations is the continuous feather cover, which contrasts with the alternating pattern of feather tracts and featherless strips of skin typical for most other birds. For diving the penguin's bones have to be heavier than the air-filled skeleton of a flying bird, and its wings have been "redesigned" to become flippers for underwater flight. A thick layer of blubber aids the penguin's thermoregulation, and salt glands excrete excess salt that the bird takes in with sea water. The olfactory lobe is large, and olfaction may be more developed than generally assumed.

Antarctic penguins have elaborated a number of these general adaptations. They are able to fast for several weeks, have a thick layer of blubber, and feathers cover their bills and feet. They nest closely together, thus making the best use of scarce ice-free areas. The emperor penguin has carried these features to an extreme, and no longer needs solid land for any phase of its life cycle.

## ANATOMICAL ADAPTATIONS
## TO THE POLAR CLIMATE

Emperor and Adélie penguins have colonized the most extreme latitudes. The emperor is the largest of all penguins, weighs 30 kg, and measures one meter from the tip of the bill to the base of the tail. A large body has relatively less surface area than a small one, and therefore has a thermoregulatory advantage in a cold climate; among related species or subspecies, the larger forms are generally found closer to the poles (Bergmann's rule). In addition to body size, the dense plumage and a thick layer of blubber guarantee optimal insulation from the environmental temperatures.

If we compare emperor and king penguins, we find two more adaptations in the former. Feathers cover the bill and feet more extensively than in the king penguin. In the emperor penguin, only the toes are visible, while there are no feathers on the tarsus-metatarsus of the king penguin. Similarly, among the long-tailed (*Pygoscelis*) penguins, the antarctic Adélie penguin has a more feathered bill than the subantarctic gentoo penguin.

Penguins of extreme latitudes have comparatively shorter flippers than the more northern species: among the pygoscelids the more northerly gentoo penguin has longer extremities than the Adélie penguin. This relationship between relative size of body appendages and climate is known as Allen's rule. Also, the foot of the subantarctic king penguin is much larger than that of the extremely Antarctic emperor penguin.

The heavy layer of blubber in the emperor penguin not only provides insulation, but is a vital energy reserve: During the 2–4 month fast of the males they may lose as much as 20 kg body weight (Prévost 1961).

## BEHAVIORAL ADAPTATIONS
## TO THE POLAR CLIMATE

Emperor penguins often save energy by moving as little as possible. I observed a molting emperor penguin at Cape Hallett that stood on the same spot on top of an ice block for 23 days. The fledging emperor chicks need not move to leave their colony, since the colony is located on the sea ice, and the ice will break up. The young penguins use the newly formed ice floes to travel northward, aided by winds and currents. This breakup occurs in summer, around December. There is also no need to climb slopes, since the whole life cycle of the emperor penguin takes place at sea level. (As an exception, they may climb ice shelves, such as the Ross Ice Shelf at Cape Crozier.) Dissipation of heat after exertion would be a greater problem for the heavily insulated emperor penguin than conservation of heat.

An impressive adaptation to the Antarctic climate is the social thermoregulation of the emperor penguin, described by Prévost and Bourlière in 1957. Incubating males have to withstand temperatures ranging from

−5° C to −30° C, aggravated by wind velocities up to 200 km/h. They not only tolerate each other without signs of territoriality but huddle together so closely that their heat loss is decreased considerably. The cloacal temperature of the tightly packed birds is 2° C lower, on average, than that of birds standing singly. Birds in the huddle lose only half as much weight as single individuals. Only ⅙ of the body surface of the grouped penguins is exposed to the wind. It has been estimated that a breeding male uses up 15% of its energy reserves for walking 100 km to the rookery and back. The remaining 85% is needed for thermoregulation. In the absence of huddling this need would exceed the available energy (Pinchow et al. 1976).

The eggs of Adélie penguins on their cold rock surface cool fast, and have to be turned more often than those of birds of temperate latitudes. The lower surface may be as much as 4° C colder than the upper surface that is in contact with the parent bird's brood patch (Todd pers. comm.).

# Chapter 9

# MAN AND PENGUIN_____

The early sealers, whalers and explorers appreciated penguin rookeries as sources of fresh meat and eggs. For instance, in 1858 sealers on Heard Island used skins of king penguins for clothing and their blubber for fuel (Crowther 1970). Even in the twentieth century Antarctic penguins have provided emergency food for Antarctic expeditions. A particularly dramatic example of this occurred during Sir Ernest Shackleton's expedition (1914–1917), when his vessel *Endurance* was lost in the Weddell Sea and 22 men had to wait on Elephant Island for four and a half months before being rescued.

Really devastating for the penguin rookeries, however, has been commercial egg collecting. On Dassen Island, off the west coast of South Africa, 300,000 eggs of the black-footed penguin were sold annually (Sparks and Soper 1967). On the Falkland Islands gentoo penguins provided large numbers of eggs during the traditional "egging week" around November 9 (Strange 1981). On one day as many as 13,000 rockhopper penguin eggs have been collected, and the Falklanders consumed 61 penguin eggs per head annually. Still today penguins provide fresh eggs on the Falklands, with an annual take of 10,000. While in the past whole rookeries of the rockhopper penguins were decimated, the current collecting is based on sound biology, and the penguins are given a chance to replace the eggs taken.

Figure 2.   Abandoned digesters on Macquarie Island, used for rendering royal penguins around 1900.

The king penguin has especially suffered from exploitation, being large and hence a profitable quarry. On the Falkland Islands the last colony was reportedly exterminated to make oil for sealing roofs. By 1945 they started breeding again, and today there are 4 small colonies (Strange 1981). On South Georgia, 20th-century sealers and whalers preferred to collect the eggs of the king penguin. On Macquarie Island king penguins were rendered after the fur seals and the blubber-rich elephant seals had been exterminated. The king penguins had been depleted, the royal penguins were slaughtered. Every year as many as 150,000 royal penguins were "processed" within a 6-week period. After 25 years of operation under license from Tasmania, the penguin harvesting was terminated. The public resented the slaughter, especially since rumors circulated that the penguins were driven alive into the cookers. The oil cookers can still be seen today (Fig. 2). Peterson (1978) has discussed the interactions of penguins with man.

Today tropical penguins in South America and South Africa are economically important only as a source of guano, and penguins of the Antarctic and subantarctic as tourist attractions. For the Antarctic, the conservation of living resources is generally accepted. Appendices III–VIII to the 1959 Antarctic Treaty prohibit "killing, wounding, capturing or molesting of any native mammal or native bird or any attempt at any such act, except in accordance with a permit" (*Agreed Measures for the Conservation of Antarctic Fauna and Flora,* Article VI).

Every specimen (animal or egg) collected with a collecting permit for scientific purposes has to be approved by and reported to SCAR (Scientific Committee for Antarctic Research) committees. Increasing traffic by tourists, scientists, research station and military personnel poses new hazards. Repeated disturbances of the breeding behavior of Antarctic penguins by naive amateur photographers, and even more so by helicopter overflights, may lead to considerable losses of eggs and chicks by breakage, exposure and predation.

Today, as during the "heroic age" of Antarctic exploration, no expedition report is complete without anecdotes or pictures of the encounter between man and penguin.

In zoos penguins are always a particular attraction, especially if they are kept well enough to breed successfully. In the Edinburgh Zoo gentoo, king and rockhopper penguins breed, and the zoo even exports penguins. Every afternoon the Edinburgh Zoo holds a "Penguin Parade," where all 3 species follow the keeper round the zoo.

Hubbs Sea World in San Diego keeps a large number of penguins, and currently (1982) 50–60 Adélie chicks are raised annually. In 1980 the first 3 emperor chicks hatched in captivity and were raised there (Fig. 3), and in 1981 2 more. In 1982 another 2 hatched, of which 1 was hand raised (Frank Todd pers. comm.).

Figure 3.   First emperor penguin chick hatched in captivity; Hubbs Sea World Research Institute.

Currently 2 tourist ships make cruises to the Antarctic and suban-tarctic, with penguins as the main attraction, ranking before seals, glaciers or icebergs. Besides fishing (for Antarctic "cod" and krill), these cruises are at present the only economic exploitation of the Antarctic, totaling about 10 million U.S. dollars annually.

Oil pollution poses a danger for northern penguin species. In South Africa, 87% of jackass penguins that were cleaned with detergent or liquid paraffin after oil-spills returned to their colony, and many of them bred. This justified the cleaning effort (Randall et al. 1980). The 1983 spill of 73 million gallons of crude oil from the supertanker *Castillo de Bellver* off Saldanha Bay, South Africa, underscores the continued threat that major shipping lanes pose to penguin colonies.

The most recent counts of breeding populations of pygoscelid pen-guins in the area of the Antarctic Peninsula show that some colonies have decreased in size, while others have increased. As far as we know, human activity is correlated with the decline of the numbers of breeding penguins. Rookeries that have been severely disturbed, or are visited frequently, have suffered losses, while others in more remote areas have not only thrived, but grown, in some cases spectacularly, regardless of species.

Table 2 lists a few examples of documented population changes. Declines seem to have occurred among the Adélies at Torgersen Island which is frequently visited by Palmer Station scientists and support per-sonnel; the same thing has happened to the chinstrap and gentoo penguins at Waterboat Point, where the Chilean station Gonzalez Videla has been built and periodically reopened. Increases, on the other hand, are seen at rookeries that are off the beaten path of tourists and scientists, such as Entrance Point at Deception Island (chinstraps), Harmony point on Nel-son Island (chinstraps and gentoos) and Danco Island in the Errara Chan-nel (gentoos). The gentoo penguins at Port Lockroy, which is visited regularly, but not as often as Torgersen Island, have been holding their own.

Although the correlation does not prove causal connection, it is highly suggestive. Therefore every precaution should be taken not to dis-turb penguins. This includes: avoiding rookery visits before the birds are established in their territories at the beginning of the breeding season (October-November); not approaching nests closer than 5 meters; limiting sightseeing to designated areas of specific tourist interest, rather than dis-tributing such visits irregularly among many rookeries.

Just as frequent human visitation can discourage penguins from re-turning to their colonies, so can this trend be reversed by strictly curbing visits and keeping visitors at a distance from the breeding birds. This has been demonstrated at the Adélie penguin rookery at Cape Royds, the southernmost penguin rookery in the world, at 77° 32'S.

Table 2.  Recent numbers of Pygoscelid Penguins in some rookeries of the Antarctic Peninsula Area

| Location | Number | Date visited | Conversion to no. of nests at start of incuba-tion (mid-Nov.) | Previous Count | | Author* | Change | |
| --- | --- | --- | --- | --- | --- | --- | --- | --- |
| | | | | Number of Nests | Date | | % | period (years) |
| ADELIE P. | | | | | | | | |
| Torgersen I. | 6500 chicks | 27 Jan. 1982 | 6566[a] | 8650[e] | 2 Dec. 1971 | MS | −24 | 10 |
| " | 5523 nests | 2 Jan. 1983 | 7890[b] | " | " | | −36 | 11 |
| " | 5575 nests | 30 Dec. 1983 | 7964[b] | | | | −9 | 12 |
| CHINSTRAP P. | | | | | | | | |
| Waterboat Point: Coal Pt. | 60 nests | 28 Dec. 1980 | na | 350 | 1 Jan. 1922 | B | −83 | 59 |
| Waterboat South I. and The Island | 2 nests | " | na | 225 | " | B | −99 | 59 |
| | | | | 125 | 1964 | C | −98 | 16 |
| Deception I.: Entrance Pt. | 1464 chicks | 25 Jan. 1982 | 1331[c] | 450 | 9 Jan. 1965 | C | +207 | 17 |
| GENTOO P. | | | | | | | | |
| Port Lockroy: Alice Creek | 562 nests | 28 Dec. 1980 | ? | 740[e] | 7 Dec. 1971 | MS | about −20 | 9 |
| " | 917 chicks | 26 Jan. 1982 | 819[d] | " | " | | +11 | 10 |
| " | 872 nests | 31 Dec. 1983 | ? | " | | MS | +18 | 11 |

| Location | | | | | | | | |
|---|---|---|---|---|---|---|---|---|
| Waterboat Pt.: Coal Pt. | 153 nests | 28 Dec. 1980 | na | 6000 | 1922 | B | −91 | 59 |
| Waterboat South I., and The Island | 387 nests | 28 Dec. 1980 | na | 450 | 1964 | C | −14 | 16 |
| Nelson Island: Harmony Pt. | 1514 nests | 30 Dec. 1982 | na | 800 | Dec. 1971/ Jan. 1972 | MS | +89 | 11 |
| Danco Island | 453 nests | 31 Dec. 1982 | na | 229 | 15 Dec. 1971 | MS | +98 | 11 |

B: Bagshawe (1938);   C = Croxall and Kirkwood (1979);   MS: Muller-Schwarze and Muller-Schwarze (1975b).

a) Assuming 45% egg + chick mortality (Oelke, 1975, range: 32–74% in Yeates' 1968 study) and an average of 1.8 eggs laid per nest (Taylor, 1962).

b) Assuming a 30% drop in the number of productive nests between mid-November and January 1 (Sladen, 1958).

c) Assuming 1.1 chick hatched per pair (Trivelpiece, 1981).

d) Assuming 1.12 chick creched per pair (Trivelpiece, 1981).

e) Negligible nest loss between mid-November and beginning of December is assumed.

Figure 4.   Man's impact: Adélies have built their nest on drifted-in fuel drum. Receding of snowdrift (left) prevents further access to nest and clutch. Cape Hallett, 1964.

This rookery is located close to the large U.S. McMurdo base. Between 1956, when McMurdo Station was established, and 1963, the number of nests dropped from 2000 to about half that. There had been visits by personnel and VIPs "almost every fine day," and on some days up to four parties of visitors arrived (Stonehouse 1965).

From 1963, access to the rookery was restricted, and from 1966 no research was carried out. Beginning in 1969, 2 New Zealand caretaker/rangers were stationed at Cape Royds during the peak visitor period in November and December. Helicopter landings in or near the rookery were banned, and visitors were kept at least 3 m from the penguins. This management scheme worked: within 10 years the rookery had recovered to 1700 nests (Thomson 1977). By now should have reached its original level.

Competition by man for the few ice-free promontories in the Antarctic directly affects the behavior and ecology of local wildlife. Original nesting grounds may be covered by buildings or stored materials (Fig. 4). Predators and scavengers such as South Polar skuas may be provisioned at stations (Fig. 5) and/or forage at garbage dumps. This alters their migrations, their breeding success, and distracts them from their natural habit of feeding at sea or in the penguin rookeries—which may possibly in turn affect penguin breeding success.

Figure 5.   Man's impact: South Polar skuas being fed steak from galley at Hallett Station (now closed).

# Part II.

_____THE PENGUIN SPECIES

# Chapter 1

# THE ADELIE PENGUIN _____

## PHYSICAL FEATURES

The adult Adélie penguin is about 70 cm long and weighs 5–6 kg. The head, including cheeks and throat, is black, as are the back and the long tail which is 16–17.8 cm long and consists of 14 feathers on the average. The upper side, tip and leading edge of the flippers are black. Neck, chest and abdomen are creamy white. Unique is the white eye-ring formed by the eye lids. The bill is short (about 5.6 cm long), is black on top and on the sides, and yellow-brown on the tip and lower mandible. The soft corners of the bill and the tongue are pink, and the inside is brown, with pink lamellae. The dorsal side of the feet is yellow-waxy with black or horn-colored toe-nails, and the ventral side is blackish. The cloaca is pink.

Newly hatched Adélie chicks have a dense down plumage. Most of the body is silver-gray, and the head is dark, almost black. There are three color phases, ranging from dark to light. Gradually the chicks develop a uniformly blackish grey down cover at about 2–3 weeks of age. The second molt starts at the age of 8 weeks and results in the typical coat with a white ventral side and a dark back. For some time, gray feathers of the whisp of down on the head and neck are left, reminiscent of a baroque wig. The two-month-old fledglings have—in contrast to the adults—a white throat; they lack the white eye-ring, the beak is all black, and they are smaller than adults. Yearlings have a white eye-ring, but still the white throat.

## SEASONAL MIGRATIONS

The Adélie penguin spends its entire life south of the northern edge of the pack ice. Occasionally individuals have been seen as far north as South Georgia. During the austral summer the Adélie breeds on the coasts of the Antarctic continent and islands. At the end of the breeding season it migrates north, and stays where two requirements are met: open water for foraging, and ice floes for resting. Hence, the pack ice belt between the fast ice near the continent and the open ocean in the north is the home of the Adélie penguin during the 8 months it is not breeding.

The spring migration south to the breeding grounds is a social affair. In October, groups numbering up to several hundreds walk in single file over the continuous sea ice. They prefer the thicker "white" ice and higher ice piles produced by the collisions of ice floes. They stop at the edge of thin ("gray") ice, and single penguins cross these patches, running quickly. They also may rest and sleep for hours at the boundary between the two types of ice, as they do when encountering an open lead between ice floes. While the penguins wait, the lead or thin ice often freezes enough to enable them to walk across it. Especially during calm nights this happens regularly. Wind and currents may also close a gap between ice fields. Waiting is thus an important part of the Adélie penguin's strategy of migration and pre-dator-avoidance. If continuous ice extends in a direction different from that of their migration, Adélies will move on and be temporarily deflected from their true direction.

The northward migration starts in February. Then the young have fledged, beach and sea have little ice, and the birds swim from the rookery or drift away on ice floes. The young gather at the beach, where their departure is facilitated by adult groups, although they are unable to keep pace with the adults. Therefore they are forced to migrate north independently of the adults.

## ORIENTATION

Adélie penguins return to the same rookery, even the same nest, year after year. Even young birds that have been at sea for several years, return to the vicinity of their natal nest and carry out their first breeding attempts (LeResche and Sladen 1970). Adélies that were experimentally displaced from Wilkes Station to McMurdo returned to their original rookery near Wilkes. They had covered 3800 km in less than 10 months, partly swimming, partly walking. This is a daily average of 13 km (Penney and Emlen 1967).

This impressive homing ability indicates that Adélies must possess very precise navigation mechanisms. Long-range orientation during migration probably uses celestial bodies, while orientation in the rookery and finding of the nest site may be guided by landmarks. Olfactory orientation in relation to the guano odor from rookeries cannot be ruled out.

Emlen and Penney (1964) displaced Adélie penguins from the coast into the featureless interior of Antarctica, in order to test the orientational abilities in the absence of landmarks. They found that Adélies head north northeast toward the coast, in a well oriented fashion, as long as the sun shines. Under overcast skies they become erratic or stopped walking. Even Adélies that were displaced into the pack ice to the north of their coastal rookeries left the release site in a NNE direction. The same happened at the South Pole. Here the sun altitude does not change during the course of a day, and could thus be excluded as a cue for the penguins. Birds from Mirny Station, 2700 km and 88 degrees of longitude to the "west", initially headed NW, but after 3 weeks of detention at the new site, they chose a NNE direction, even more pronounced than the local (Ross Sea) Adélies. A northern course would bring a penguin back to the coast and its food sources if it had been accidentally displaced inland. The east component of the NNE departure direction of displaced penguins is interpreted as compensation for the predominantly east to west currents and winds that would deflect a penguin to the west were it to maintain a strictly south-north course when traveling between rookery and pack ice (Penney and Emlen 1967). Later, Penney and Riker (1969) found that Adélies that had been transferred to the northern hemisphere calculated the sun's path there (from east to south to west) the wrong way, i.e., they expected the sun to move from east to north to west.

## BREEDING BIOLOGY*
*Arrival*

In mid-October, the Antarctic spring, Adélie penguins come in groups of often hundreds from the pack-ice to their familiar rookeries. On fast ice they walk or toboggan, and in open water they use ice floes as vehicle whenever possible. Because of the danger of leopard seal attacks, they walk around open leads or thin patches of ice, or run or leap over them as fast as possible. In open water they "porpoise," change to swimming "duck-style" near the beach, and jump ashore with a vertical leap.

Males arrive first in the rookery, followed by the females several days later. Older individuals arrive before young ones (LeResche and Sladen

---

*While this book was in press, the comprehensive review of breeding behavior of Adélie penguins by Ainley et al. (1983) appeared. It summarizes earlier papers that are quoted here, and also adds new population data.

Figure 6.    Adélie penguin nests on knolls that were snow-free at the time of nest building. Gentoo penguins in foreground. Stranger Point, King George Island.

1970). The youngest come so late that they cannot form a pair, are unable to obtain a good breeding territory, and thus do not participate in breeding.

Upon arrival, the males shake their feathers, preen, eat snow and walk up the slope to the area where they had nested the previous year. Since it is early in the season, most of the terrain is still snow-covered. Open, windswept knolls and ridges are the only areas available for building nests (Fig. 6). If a male finds another male already occupying his former nest site, a short, but severe fight will ensue. They bite into each other's bill, flail the opponent with the flippers and finally one chases the other over several meters. The victor returns to his territory. Knowledge of the terrain, age, experience and hormonal state all seem to contribute to the superiority of one male over the other.

*Nest building*

The male lies down on his abdomen, and scrapes a depression with his feet, using them alternately or synchronously. Some time later he begins to collect nest material. Pebbles, ranging in size from 1 to 5 cm diameter are picked up with the bill and quickly carried to the nest site. Often one

Figure 7   A particularly large nest of the Adélie penguin. Cape Hallett, Victorialand.

Figure 8    Female (on right) responds to male's Ecstatic Display by bringing a pebble.

Figure 9    Female responds to Ecstatic Display by male with Quiet Mutual Display.

**Figure 10**   Loud Mutual Display of a pair of Adélie penguins. Note the white sclera of the eye and that flippers are held against the body.

bird will collect pebbles from the nest of another that is under construction and not closely guarded. If intercepted, the trespasser will be attacked with bill and flippers. The nests are never finished; even after the chicks have hatched, pebbles may still be added (Fig. 7). During incubation the sitting bird often rearranges the pebbles in the nest. Although initially only the male builds the nest, later both partners participate in all nest building behavior.

The mean distances between the centers of Adélie nests ranged between 67 and 84 cm in the area of the Antarctic Peninsula (Müller-Schwarze and Müller-Schwarze 1975), and at Wilkes Station (66° 15'S, 110° 32° E) 65 to 72 cm (Penney 1968).

*Courtship*

The Adélie penguins exhibits five behavior patterns during courtship that occur in similar form in related species: the "ecstatic" display, the "oblique stare bow," the "bill to axilla," and the "loud mutual" and "quiet mutual" displays.

In the "ecstatic" display the male raises the head and points its bill skyward, while the chest is protruded. During the raising of the head the flippers wave slowly and simultaneously, and the bird utters rhythmical cracking sounds (Fig. 8). The eye is rolled so that the white sclera becomes visible. As soon as the bill points us vertically, the "ecstatic" display ends with a loud shriek. This display is contagious: one displaying male may induce 5 or more birds of the same breeding group to do the same. The

Figure 11   Quiet Mutual Display of the Adélie penguin. The bills are closed, a humming sound is uttered, and the flippers are held against the body.

"ecstatic" display often interrupts nest building, especially when a female passes by. She may stop and respond with the "oblique stare bow": the head is lowered slowly and turned sideways. The male also may perform the oblique stare bow vis-a-vis a strange female. It is the opposite of attack: the bill is closed and turned away from the other penguin. Females that are paired already, respond to the "ecstatic" display with the "quiet mutual" display (Fig. 9; see below).

The third display is the "bill-to-axilla". It is typical for males, but females sometimes perform it too. The bird keeps his body at an angle of about 45° with the ground, and the closed bill points to the base of the flipper (axilla), while the head is turned around its long axis in both directions. The white sclera of the eye becomes visible during this display. Simultaneously with the head turns, slow sounds are uttered that can be rendered as "oarrr-oarrr-oarrr".

Birds of opposite gender greet each other with the "loud mutual" display if they know each other from the previous breeding season. Both partners point their heads up vertically, with feathers on the nape of the neck erected, open the bill, wave their heads back and forth and utter a series of loud cackling calls (Fig. 10). The "quiet mutual" display consists also of head raising and waving, but the bills are closed and a soft humming sound can be heard. At the same time the flippers are held tightly against the body, and the feathers of the crest are raised (Fig. 11).

Ainley (1975) has re-interpreted the various displays of the Adélie penguiin.

### Pair Bond

We distinguish two levels of pair bonding: trial pairing and true pairing. The former is temporary and does not lead to egg-laying although the birds copulate, while the latter results in a clutch and lasts through the entire breeding season, culminating in the raising and fledging of chicks. Both types of pairing start with the same behavior patterns, which differ only in their intensity: the female is attracted by the ecstatic display of the male, and after mutual bowing the male will lie down on its nest or nest depression, which it starts to scratch out with its feet. The female then collects pebbles and deposits them beside the male. He incorporates them into the nest. Further mutual bowing and collecting of pebbles as well as joint nest defense against trespassers lead to copulation. When copulating, the male stands on the back of the female and waves his flippers. Both partners touch and stimulate each other's bill. During the period of copulation, females often can be recognized by the muddy treadmarks on their backs.

### Breeding Behavior

The breeding behavior of Adélie penguins has been investigated thoroughly in several rookeries (Sladen 1958; Sapin-Jaloustre 1960; Tay-

Figure 12    The typical clutch of the Adélie penguin consists of 2 eggs. Note the brood patch.

lor 1962). The Adélie penguin lays two eggs (Fig. 12), on the average 1.71eggs per pair (Taylor 1962). The incubation time averages 35 days. Most egg-laying occurs in the first two weeks of November, and most chicks hatch between December 10 and 15. Egg-laying and hatching peaks vary in different rookeries in the Ross Sea, and occur earlier in the northern part of the Adélie's distribution (e.g. the South Shetland Islands).

After the second egg has been laid, the male incubates the clutch, and the female goes to sea and forages. After about two weeks the female returns and relieves the male. Now the female incubates for two weeks. During the last week of incubation the two mates relieve each other every 1–2 days.

Each nest relief is accompanied by a ceremony, consisting of loud displays. Upon meeting at the nest, the two mates perform the loud mutual display: after an initial bow, the heads are raised, the necks waved back and forth and a loud cackling is uttered with the bill open. With decreasing excitement the sounds become softer and the bills are kept closed. The heads are still waved back and forth, and a soft humming sound is uttered (the "quiet mutual" display). This display is not always "mutual": the partner may not join in, or a male may perform it at arrival at his empty nest bowl, but also when seeing his egg, especially when just laid. It may also be directed at a chick which may or may not reciprocate.

The incubating Adélie lies prone in the depression on top of the pile of pebbles that forms the nest (Fig. 7). He covers the eggs with his heavily vascularized brood patch, an abdominal area that loses its feathers prior to incubation.

The shell of the Adélie penguin's egg is thick ($\bar{x}$ = 0.644 ± 0.05 microns; N = 9) compared with that of chicken eggs ($\bar{x}$ = 0.347 ± 0.03 microns; N = 9). The weight of Adelie eggs may average 111.6 ± 10.8 grams (Sladen 1958), but the shell thickness corresponds to an egg weighing over 200 grams (Ar et al. 1974).

When incubating, Adélies face the wind. Since reclining penguins squirt their droppings over the nest's edge, one can read the prevailing wind direction during the preceding days from the direction of the white guano lines. Fasting penguins have greenish-white feces; the color changes to salmon-pink or orange after they have been foraging on krill, or to white if they have fed on fish. This is a clue as to whether or not a nest relief has taken place recently.

The females start to breed when 3 years old, the males as four-year-olds. Some birds may not breed until they are 7 years old (LeResche and Sladen 1970).

The number of adult penguins present in the rookery reaches a maximum around November 15. It declines until mid-December, since many birds loose their clutch, and the females go to sea. A second peak in numbers is reached during the so-called "reoccupation period" at the beginning of January (Sladen 1958; Spurr 1977). It is therefore recommended that ground and aerial counts of breeding Adélie penguins be carried out on or around November 15.

*Raising the Young*

At hatching, the chicks of the Adélie penguin weigh 80–90 grams and are covered with a soft down that is silver gray on the body, and black on the head. The broken egg shell is ignored by the parent birds and carried away by the wind.

The chicks are reared in two distinct phases: the guard stage and crèche stage. The guard stage lasts about 3 weeks, and during that time the chicks never leave their nests (Figs. 13 and 14). Most of the time they

Figure 13    Feeding a chick during the guard stage: First phase: The chick begs at the lower mandible of the parent.

Figure 14    Feeding, second phase: The adult leans forward and regurgitates food which the chick takes by inserting its bill into that of the adults.

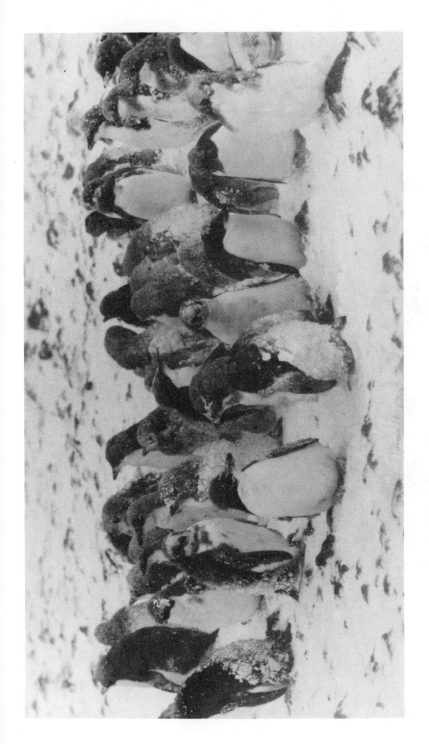

Figure 15   A crèche of molting Adélie chicks in a blizzard.

Figure 16   Feeding Run: During the crèche stage Adélies feed their young in neutral areas. The parent bird runs away from the crèche, and the chicks follow. One chick is fed as soon as foreign chicks have been warded off and their own chicks have separated.

are covered by the parent's brood patch, or, when older, the head at least is tucked under the brooding adult. Like gull chicks, penguin chicks are nidiculous, i.e. intermediate between altricial and precocial birds: The chick is protected and defended against neighbors and skuas by the parents. It does not move from the nest, but is fully covered with down when hatching. Large chicks are protected from strong winds by standing in the lee of the adult. They can thermoregulate from an age of about 15 days.

The crèche stage starts at the age of 3 weeks. The chicks leave their nests and join neighbor chicks to form groups (Fig. 15). The nest quickly deteriorates from trampling and lack of further maintenance. Gradually the crèches grow from 2 to 3 chicks to as many as 20, or even 30. These dense groups provide wind protection and are immune against skuas, even in the absence of adults, although skuas would be physically capable of removing chicks from crèches. Isolated chicks will be attacked immediately.

In the crèches the parents feed only their own young. An adult, upon returning from the sea, walks to the crèche, stops at his now deserted nest site, and calls with a "loud mutual" display. This attracts his or her chicks, and sometimes also one or several other chicks, and they start to beg for food. Play-back experiments with tape recordings demonstrated that the chicks recognize their parents by their voice (Penney 1968). The adult does not feed yet, and starts the second part of the feeding ritual: it runs away from the begging young and the crèche. This is the "feeding run" or "feeding chase", (Fig. 16). Initially, this "feeding run" covers only 1–2 meters, later it may be 50 meters. The begging young follow. In most cases the strange chicks stay behind, and the penguin's own young persist. If they stop running and lag behind, the parent bird stops, turns around, returns to them and then the begging and running starts anew. If both chicks beg at the same time when the adult stops, he will peck them. The chicks then duck flat on the ground. Only after the chicks are strung out and only one begs, will the adult start to regurgitate food and feed it. Parents with only one young usually do not show this "feeding run." The main function of this behavior seems to be the separation of the young, so that one can be fed at a time, thus minimizing the risk of loosing precious food during the vigorous competition of two begging chicks. Additional benefits of the "feeding run" may accrue to the chicks: they exercise their locomotor abilities, familiarize themselves with new terrain and learn to negotiate it. Encounters with other crèches and adults provide social experience, since the chicks are attacked quite often. All the while the parent bird is present, protecting the chick(s) from attacks by skuas.

By the first week of February, the chicks have molted to a blue/black-and-white plumage. The parents stop feeding them, and they move downhill and gather at the beach (Fig. 17). While at the beach, they climb ice blocks and compete vigorously for a space on the top. They even climb on Weddell seals. This behavior is a pre-adaptation for life at sea, when

Figure 17    Eight-week old Adélie chicks have gathered at the beach to leave the rookery. Their throats are white, and whisps of down are left on head and back.

ice floes and bergs provide rest and safety from leopard seals and, possibly, killer whales. We have also observed play behavior while the chicks are waiting at the beach: They run suddenly, waving their flippers, making sudden turns, bump and peck each other, cock-fight fashion (Müller-Schwarze 1978). Facilitated by the departure of noisy groups of adults, the chicks enter the surf, but may retreat to the beach. When they finally leave, they swim and paddle awkwardly, vocalizing all the time. They swim out into the ocean without accompanying adults, and at this time are most vulnerable to leopard seal predation (see p. 000).

## MORTALITY

The egg and chick losses during the time between egg-laying and the exodus from the rookery (fledging) can range from 32.5% and 43% (Yeates 1968) to 60 and 82% (Sladen 1958). Sapin-Jaloustre (1960) recorded 68% mortality. Early and late breeders are most likely to lose eggs and chicks due to failure to relieve the mate in time (Davis 1982). Severe storms are often the main source of chick mortality. By comparison, the loss among altricial birds in temperate latitudes ranges from 40 to 60% (Nice 1957). Northern penguin species often have much higher egg and chick mortality (see pp. 142, 161 and 168).

At 7–8 years, Adélie penguins have reached the age at which they are most efficient at raising chicks. Thirty-six percent of 7–8 year old pairs raise two-chick broods successfully. By comparison, three-year-olds raise 0%, and four-year-olds 8% two-chick broods. Chicks in one-chick broods are heavier than those in two-chick broods. The former weigh 3.3 kg at fledging, the latter 3.1 kg (Ainley and Schlatter 1972). Adélies with two chicks bring less than twice the food that parents of one chick obtain from the ocean (Emison 1968).

## FIGHTING AND THREATENING: AGONISTIC BEHAVIOR

Colonial birds need mechanisms that prevent strife and friction. Avoidance of confusion, interference with brooding or feeding, injury or death to eggs and chicks, and unnecessary energy expenditure are particularly vital under the extreme conditions under which the Adélies raises their young. It is not surprising to find behavior patterns that make it possible to rear young successfully in crowded colonies, and we may suppose that mere threatening serves as a substitute for actual fighting in social encounters between territory owners.

The nests of the Adélie penguin are usually spaced such that the territory owners just reach each other with the tips of their bills. The distances between the centers of nests are 65–72 cm at the Wilkes (now Casey) Station (Penney 1968) and 67–84 cm in four different rookeries

Figure 18   Figure Large colonies of Adélies at Point Thomas, on King George Island (South Shetland Islands).

in the area of the Antarctic Peninsula (Müller-Schwarze and Müller-Schwarze 1975). The Adélie penguins breed closer together than the other two *Pygoscelis* species. We measured mean minimum inter-nest distances of 86 cm for the chinstrap penguin, and 101 cm for the gentoo, both in the Antarctic Peninsula area. This ability to nest close together can be seen as an adaptation to an extreme austral habitat, where ice-free space is not only at a premium but may also vary unpredictably from year to year due to fluctuations of snowfall and the rate of thawing.

The first sign of agonistic behavior by an Adélie on his nest is erection of the feathers on the nape of the neck and a lateral turn of the head, which Penney (1968) called the "oblique stare," with the white sclera of the eye showing. With increasing readiness to fight the bill is opened and a guttural sound uttered. Finally, the attack follows: the bill moves forward, and the flippers are lifted. The opponent is grabbed with the bill, and flailed with the flippers. There are four situations that can lead to fighting: A bird's routine walk to its own nest through neighboring territories; competition for nest or mate at the beginning of the breeding season; disturbance (trespassing) by non-breeders; and interspecific encounters, as with skuas. Humans, when too close to breeding territories, will also be pecked and beaten with the flippers.

The frequent trips between nest and sea force food gathering parents to cross other territories, particularly when breeding in the center of large colonies. Such birds have no choice but to trespass, and they are pecked by territory holders on both sides of their path. Such "gauntlet running" may have to be undertaken through territories many rows deep. On King George Island in the South Shetlands we found an extensive colony, where the center birds had to cross up to 90 territories (Fig. 18). When "running the gauntlet" a penguin becomes as sleek as possible, with flippers held tightly against the body. He walks through as fast as possible, and keeps the bill up and away from other penguins, the most inoffensive posture. In some large colonies the center has been vacated, resulting in a doughnut-shaped pattern of occupation. We assume that avoidance of social friction led to this arrangement, although the central nests would have enjoyed the best protection from skuas.

Birds on neighboring nests often fight with short bill stabs while vocalizing harshly, or grab each others bills, and twist and pull. They remain lying flat during these exchanges (Fig. 19).

Competition for nest sites or mates often leads to vigorous fights, even between females. Typically, the male arrives first in the rookery and occupies a site which it defends as territory and advertises with the "ecstatic" display. The female arrives several days later and pair formation proceeds rapidly. Mature Adélies form pairs with the same partner in subsequent years. But if a female is delayed, her former partner will have associated with a new female, and a serious fight between the two females

Figure 19   Fighting Adélie penguins. Each bird occupies a nest, the left with eggs, the right with chicks. The bill of one bird is turned 90° in relation to that of the other. The bills rarely touch ("air cushion fighting").

may ensue. Which of the two females will prevail depends on the progress made with courtship, mating and egg-laying. A male will breed with a new female if his former partner is delayed by 5–7 days. If a female arrives before her mate, she will pair up with a new male, and after 2–3 days the male of the previous year has hardly a chance to form a bond with her. This tight schedule is an important adaptation to the short Antarctic summer, where every breeding day is a precious resource the penguins cannot afford to waste.

Disturbances by non-breeding Adélies also trigger agonistic behavior. This happens when immature birds or some of those who have lost their clutches trespass into breeding territories or are attracted by certain stimulus situations. For instance, "bachelors" often try to copulate with chicks that are lying flat on the ground. Such disturbances typically trigger "loud mutual" displays in a breeding pair (Fig. 20).

Interspecific threats and fights, such as occur vis-a-vis skuas, employ the same behavior patterns that are used in intraspecific encounters. A skua that tries to land in or at a colony, faces a "forest of bills" pointing at it. At very close range, the bills directed at the skua are open, but closed at distances of more than one meter. Bills pointed up at skuas do not threaten other penguins. More details and experimental results are given in the chapter on predators and anti-predator behavior (p. 84).

In late January non-breeders and unsuccessful breeders return from the sea to the rookery to defend territories and form pairs. The selective advantage of this behavior is to develop an early claim to a breeding site for the following season under the conditions of limited breeding space. Penguins that have stayed at least 10 days at a particular nest site with a particular partner during the reoccupation period are most likely to return to the same site and breed with the same partner in the following season (Spurr 1977).

In its aggressive behavior the Adélie penguin is intermediate between chinstrap and gentoo penguins. The chinstrap attacks conspecifics and humans vigorously, while gentoos flee easily from their nests when a person approaches. But during nest relief ceremonies we observed more frequent aggressive behavior patterns in the Adélie penguin than in the other two species.

## ACTIVITY RHYTHMS

The activity rhythm of Adélie penguins has been investigated only during the breeding season (Müller-Schwarze 1968; Yeates 1971). During the continuous daylight of the austral summer Adélies maintain a clear diurnal cycle of activity as known for day-active animals. Activity intensifies particularly between 4:00 and 10:00 a.m., when the light intensity increases rapidly. After that, the activity decreases until it reaches a minimum around

Figure 20   Loud Mutual Display during an agonistic encounter between two Adélie pairs. Note the white sclera in center bird.

midnight. Behaviors following this general pattern are the ecstatic display, walking to and from the rookery, and the activity of the chicks. These observations were made at Hallett Station (72° 19′S, 170° 13′E) and have been confirmed for other parts of the Ross Sea, such as Cape Royds (77° 23′S, 166° 09′E: Yeates 1971) or Cape Crozier (77° 3′S, 169° 23′E), and in the area of the Antarctic Peninsula (62° to 67° S). The light intensities vary from 300 lux at "night" to 60,000 lux during midday at Hallett, but on the South Shetland Islands (about 62° S) there is a short true night during mid-summer, when the light intensity drops to below 0.5 lux. Then all penguin traffic to and from the beach comes to a standstill. With a typical daily maximum of 100,000 lux, the light intensity at the South Shetland Islands varies by a factor of 200,000, compared with one of 200 at Cape Hallett. Accordingly, the rhythm of daily activity is much more pronounced at the South Shetlands.

The described daily activity pattern is an adaptation to several environmental factors, such as availability of food at different times of the day (vertical migrations of plankton and plankton-dependent organisms!) thermoregulatory requirements (danger of overheating during activity in midday), or activity of predators, such as the leopard seal. The diurnal activity cycle is not completely rigid: it can be drastically altered by severe storms.

## PREDATORS AND ANTIPREDATOR BEHAVIOR

In the continental Antarctic, the typical range of Adélie penguin, the predators are the leopard seal (*Hydrurga leptonyx*, Gk.: "slender dark water worker"; Fig. 21) and the South Polar skua (*Catharacta maccormicki*; Gk.: "cleaning up," i.e. scavenging; McCormick: physician on the ship *Erebus* during the Ross Expedition to the Antarctic 1839–43, Fig. 25). In the area of the Antarctic Peninsula and on subantarctic islands several other bird species prey and scavenge in penguin rookeries. These are primarily the giant petrel (*Macronectes giganteus;* Gk.: "huge good swimmer") and the sheathbill (*Chionis alba;* Gk.: "snow-white"; Lat.: "white").

It is difficult to distinguish predation from scavenging. The avian predators mentioned above scavenge first at the beach and in the colonies, and kill only if no carcasses or addled eggs are available. One particular individual can be a scavenger now and a predator at the next meal. With eggs as food items the distinction between predation and scavenging becomes completely blurred: an addled egg outside the nest is carrion, while an egg with a living embryo is prey if killed by the skuas. Only the latter is an individual removed by skua predation. For the observer it is often impossible to determine into which class an egg falls that is carried away by a skua from a penguin colony.

Under the austere conditions of the continental Antarctic predators have to remain flexible and opportunistic, and cannot afford to specialize.

Figure 21   Leopard seal.

The South Polar skua, for instance, kills penguin chicks, but has no specific behavior patterns or techniques for killing, as found in birds of prey or carnivorous mammals. It does not hold the prey with its foot, which is webbed and unsuited for that task. It literally eats its prey alive. Skuas also catch surface fish, and presumably live exclusively on these during the southern winter. Thus, this selection pressure prevents a specialization for preying in penguin rookeries, where food is available for only 4 months of the year. (Nowadays, garbage at Antarctic stations is an important food source for the skuas).

The mortality inflicted by predators on Antarctic penguins is minor, according to the research of the past two decades. Populations are more likely to be limited by weather conditions and scarce breeding space than by predation.

*The leopard seal as predator*
The leopard seal belongs to the seals (Phocidae) which lack external ears and is distinguished from other seals by its long foreflippers, pronounced neck, and a reptile-like head, wide mouth, and powerful teeth with large canines. Adults weigh from 200 to 590 kg, with females somewhat larger. Its range is the vast Southern Ocean, and it migrates there between the subantarctic islands and the Antarctic. During the austral winter, approximately from May through November, leopard seals stay by the hundreds and thousands on subantarctic islands such as Heard and Macquarie (Gwynn 1953b; Brown 1957). During the summer many leopard seals appear at the coasts of the Antarctic continent. But only a few individuals have specialized in the exploitation of penguin rookeries as a temporary, but excellent food source. Most leopard seals live for most of the year on fish, squid, krill, other seals, etc., and even the "penguin specialists" among the leopard seals most likely feed on other marine organisms for eight of the twelve months.

Predation by leopard seals on penguins has been studied in detail only at Cape Crozier in the Ross Sea (Penney and Lowry 1967; Müller-Schwarze and Müller-Schwarze 1971, 1975). About 200,000 penguins breed at Cape Crozier, and three to six leopard seals spend the short summer near the rookery. All leopard seals that were seen clearly in that area proved to be males (Erickson pers. comm.). These are probably single pioneers that penetrate into extreme latitudes for short periods.

The hunting method of the leopard seal is to lie in wait about 20 to 500 meters off shore, and also under the overhanging ice foot. There it intercepts underwater Adélies swimming to or from the rookery. After an unsuccessful attack he does not pursue his prey, but waits for a new group to approach. Leopard seals change their position constantly. We observed individuals that we recognized by their scars on the head or back to appear at various places along landing beaches of the penguins.

Leopard seals adapt their hunting methods to the different ice conditions prevailing during the various phases of the summer season. We can distinguish four different phases during the penguins' breeding season, each requiring different hunting techniques and characterized by different rates of hunting success.

*First Phase* (October): The sea is frozen for several miles from the coast. The penguins, coming from the north, arrive on foot at their rookery. The leopard seal swims under the ice cover and pushes with his head through the ice to attack penguins (Fig. 22). He rarely catches a penguin; only 8% of the attacks are successful. An escaped penguin remains motionless—often for hours. This way he seems to be unnoticeable to the searching leopard seal under the ice.

*Second Phase* (November): The ice breaks up, and the penguins have to traverse it by alternating between walking and swimming. The ice cover opens up, solidifies, or new ice forms, depending on the ever-changing winds, temperatures, tides and currents. The leopard seal hunts in the open areas, while the penguins escape onto large ice floes. Leopard seals then often try to reach up onto ice floes to catch a penguin. Birds on small floes of two to five meters diameter may be attacked many times from different sides of the floe. They always flee to the "safe" side of the floe, but avoid the water religiously. The leopard seal sometimes pushes them off a floe.

*Third Phase* (December and January): The sea is open, only occasional ice floes drift about. The penguins "porpoise" to their feeding grounds and back to the rookery. The leopard seal patrols the beaches (Fig. 23), intercepts swimming groups close to shore, and attacks them under water. He is particularly successful at low tide, when the ice foot may be three meters above the water surface. Then the leaping penguins repeatedly fail to reach the landing area on the ice, and fall back into the water. They swim along the ice foot and try a different spot. The seal waits or cruises slowly below the ice foot and easily catches the exhausted birds. They literally fall into his mouth.

Groups that are attacked in open water, all scatter and escape in various directions, forming a splashing arc of 180°, or sometimes even a complete circle. The ripples in the center of the circle betray the leopard seal. After about 40 seconds they gather again. If the seal was successful, he will emerge after a few seconds with an Adélie in his mouth, and kill it with a powerful lateral jerk of his head, so that the penguin crashes on the water. The prey is dismembered by biting off a small piece every time the carcass is tossed on the water. While the carcass floats on the surface, the seal opens his mouth widely and swallows the meat. South Polar skuas hover about, and try to obtain morsels. Such skua activity is a sure sign of a kill.

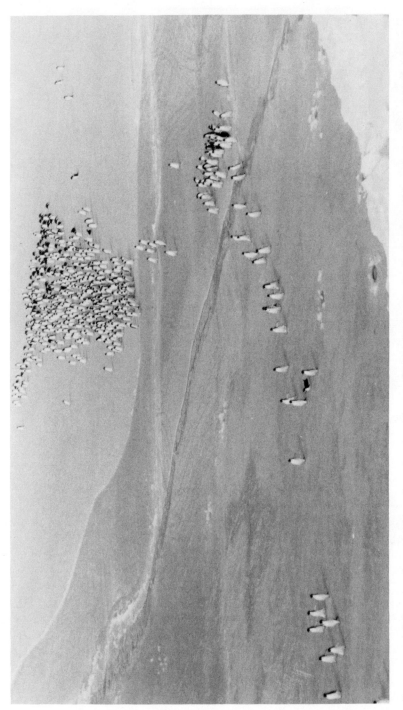

Figure 22   Adélie penguins arriving at Cape Crozier. They walk over fast ice. Holes in foreground have been created by leopard seals during attacks from under the ice.

Figure 23    Leopard seal patrolling the landing beach of the Adélie penguins. Cape Crozier, Ross Island.

*Fourth Phase* (early February): The chicks leave the rookery. The sea is still open, with only single scattered ice floes. The leopard seal eats only chicks because they are easy to catch. They swim slowly and awkwardly and are unable to dive (Fig. 24). They have no pre-programmed behavior patterns of direct predator avoidance in the water. The chicks swim toward a leopard seal just as they do toward an ice block drifting in the water. The only pre-adaptation for the dangerous life at sea is their tendency to climb ice blocks stranded on the beach prior to going to sea. They try to reach the highest point on the ice and compete vigorously with other chicks for that spot, so that some chicks are constantly falling off, while others climb to the top. We have even observed chicks climbing on top of the backs of resting Weddell seals.

After leaving the beach, the chicks still climb on any piece of ice that floats in the water in their vicinity. Often they fall off the smooth surface. If the ice floe or block is large enough, it will provide good protection against the leopard seal. But even small ice fragments floating in the sea are of advantage to the chicks, since they provide opportunities to rest and may even serve as rafts for a longer journey.

The Adélie chicks have no chance to practice swimming. The first contact with water at the beach is at the same time the start of the long migration north. The only exercise of the flippers is a dry one: a single chick may suddenly start to run around, but not in a socially synchronized or co-ordinated fashion. It may turn abruptly, and may bump into another chick. Then they will beat each other with their flippers and peck each other in a brief cock-fight. This behavior shares many features with solitary and social play that is typical for young mammals, but occurs also in other bird species (Müller-Schwarze 1978). I suggest that this "play" behavior by penguin chicks has some important adaptive function in exercising the neuromuscular apparatus, practicing social skills, or both, although no specific effects of play are known at this time for this species.

The number of penguins killed by leopard seals can be estimated. During the whole breeding season, which lasts 100 days from 23 October through 30 January, and includes all four described phases, about 4800 adult Adélies were killed by leopard seals at Cape Crozier. This is 2.4% of the adult population of approximately 200,000 birds (Butler and Müller-Schwarze 1977). For the chicks, we can also estimate the total loss. In 24 hours of observation, we saw 22 chicks killed at one of four landing beaches. During the approximately 2 weeks of the chick exodus, this would amount to 1232 chicks killed by leopard seals in one season. Assuming that each of the 100,000 breeding pairs raises 1.03 chicks successfully, 1232 of 103,000 chicks are removed by leopard seal predation. This is about 1.2% mortality. This figure may change from year to year. For instance, Penney and Lowry (1967) calculated for the same rookery at Cape Crozier about 5% mortality due to leopard seals among the adult Adélies. But mortality

Figure 24    Adélie chicks leave the rookery. Bobbing and splashing, they are inefficient swimmers. They head north in large groups and independently of adults.

due to severe storms (and locally, also flooding) is usually a more significant source of mortality, especially of eggs and chicks (Figs. 25–28).

With six leopard seals hunting at Cape Crozier, and using our data, a leopard seal obtains eight adult penguins per day, on the average, and during the chick exodus 15 chicks per day. It is safe to assume that this amount of food covers the daily requirement and no supplement of other food items is required. This means that those leopard seals that work the beaches obtain their diet easily from the rookery and are not limited by the countermeasures of the penguins. This is in contrast to the South Polar skua that often goes hungry and obtains from the rookery only one-sixth of the food it could consume (see next chapter). The nutritional require-

Figure 25   Incubating Adélie penguin after a severe snowstorm. Tightly packed snow restricts the bird's movements, so that often eggs or chicks are crushed. Only nests in poor locations will be drifted in like this. Cape Crozier.

ments of free-ranging leopard seals are difficult to determine. A male leopard seal, kept in captivity in the Taronga Zoo in Sydney, Australia, for more than six years, consumed 4.5 kg fish daily. However, the caloric intake of a seal under those conditions is lower than those that are active in the cold Antarctic waters.

Several environmental factors influence the interactions between Adélie penguins and leopard seals. One is the time of day, which is characterized by a certain level of light intensity. In the continuous polar day, the activity of the Adélies reaches its daily maximum, during the "morning" hours with their increasing light intensities while the leopard seals rest on ice floes around mid-day and are most active around midnight. Although these patterns have also thermoregulatory and other functions, it appears that the prey species tries to avoid being in the water at the same time the

Figure 26    After a severe snowstorm low-lying parts of the rookery are drifted
in. Here a completely buried nest is dug out (Cape Crozier).

leopard seal is active there. The seal, on the other hand, tracks the prey
and will be active when enough penguins are available.

Sea ice conditions determine the hunting success of the leopard seal.
Complete ice cover favors the penguins; the success rate is only 8% when
the seal has to push through the ice. By contrast, the hunting success is
greatest (92%) when the water is open, and the chicks leave the colony.
Adult penguins are caught particularly often in open water (50%), or
below the steep and over-hanging ice foot, particularly at low tide (40%).
At low tide the Adélies have to leap 3 m onto the ice foot and are easy
prey. Thus, the relationship between leopard seal and Adélie penguin is
influenced by time of day, ice conditions, and tides.

Other pinniped species also prey on penguins, although only occasionally. On the east coast of Argentina and on the Falkland Islands the
South American sea lion (*Otaria byronica*) preys on Magellanie, gentoo
and rockhopper penguins, both on land and in the water. Boswall (1972)

Figure 27     Adaptive character of Adélie's pebble nest becomes obvious during flooding by meltwater (Cape Hallett).

Figure 28    In the warmer maritime Antarctic, penguin nests can be water logged after heavy snowstorms, and many clutches will perish. Pt. Thomas, King George Island.

collected information on these incidents. Often sea lions do not eat the killed penguins. Then giant petrels consume the carcasses. At South Georgia fur seals prey on macaroni penguins. New Zealand fur seals (*Arctocephalus forsteri*) are a predator of royal penguins on Macquarie Island. Finally, in Australia, little blue penguins are killed by automobiles.

*Birds as Predators*

In the Adélie penguin rookeries of the Antarctic continent the typical predator that takes eggs and chicks is the South Polar skua (*Catharacta maccormicki*) (Fig. 29). This species' breeding biology and interactions with penguins are particularly well investigated. Therefore, this account deals with the relations between South Polar skuas and Adélie penguins.

The South Polar skua's migration pattern is similar to the Adélie penguin's: during the austral summer it breeds on the Antarctic continent and on the South Shetland and Balleny Islands. South Polar skuas probably breed in small numbers on Peter I. Island. A skua circled us when we visited that island on January 29, 1982, but no nest was seen. After the breeding season, the skuas migrate north and spend the winter in the pack ice, but range to subtropical waters, and single specimens have reached the Northern Hemisphere (Watson et al. 1971).

South Polar skuas breed mostly at the periphery of Adélie rookeries, or in the vicinity. This has led to opposing assumptions on the relationships between skuas and penguins. On the one hand, a close and obligatory dependence on the penguins for food was postulated, with the breeding of the skua following closely that of the penguin (Maher 1966). This conclusion was based on observations in the rookery at Cape Hallett, where the chicks of the skuas hatched only one week after the penguin chicks. The skuas there had available to them an optimal food base for raising their young, and did not have to go to sea, a great advantage during storms. Young (1963) arrived at an opposite conclusion. He studied the small Adélie rookery at Cape Royds, the southernmost penguin rookery in the world. There, only six of one hundred breeding skua pairs obtained their food from the rookery; the majority had to go to sea to forage. The six pairs had completely divided among themselves the rookery, which numbered about 2000 penguins. They defended these sections as feeding territories. Since only a small minority of the skuas lived on penguins, Young concluded that the skuas are not dependent on penguins. Rather, the spatial association of skua and Adélie is thought accidental. Both species merely use as breeding areas the scarce and small ice free areas close to the coast. The skuas will exploit the penguin rookery only when the opportunity exists.

Further thorough studies in other rookeries, notably at Cape Crozier in the Ross Sea, have shown that the relations between skuas and penguins vary from rookery to rookery, and lie between the two extremes discussed above. At Cape Crozier the skua chicks hatch three to four weeks after the penguins and their breeding cycle is poorly synchronized with that of the Adélies. When fast growing skua chicks require a large amount of food during the weeks after hatching, the penguin chicks are three weeks old and too large to be easy prey. They are then too heavy to be carried away, and, moreover, are gathered in crèches, where they are not attacked by skuas.

On the other hand, the spatial relationships between the two species are very close. About 950–1000 pairs of South Polar skuas nest at Cape Crozier (Wood 1971). They breed on gravel slopes above the Adélie rookery (Fig. 30) with its approximately 100,000 penguin nests. There are two categories of breeding skuas: most maintain a breeding territory around

Figure 29    South Polar skua on its nest, with 1 chick and 1 egg.

Figure 30   Part of the Adélie penguin rookery at Cape Crozier, Ross Island. Guano-stained penguin colony areas appear light; South Polar skuas breed on black gravel slopes above penguin rookery.

their nest, defending it against other skuas. The other category of skuas nest in a narrow strip along the upper edge of the penguin rookery. In addition to their nest, these 30 skua pairs defend a section of the penguin rookery as their food base. This section represents a feeding territory, and these skuas defend more complex breeding/feeding territories than those on the slopes above who only have breeding territories. At Crozier, the feeding territories extend from 32 to 91 m into the rookery, cover 726 to 2870 square m and contain from 179 to 711 penguin nests (Müller-Schwarze et al. 1975). The peripheral zone of the Adélie rookery that is thus divided into skua feeding territories, comprises about one-seventh of the total area of the rookery. The skuas keep all other conspecifics out of the feeding territories, even when there is a food surplus in the form of addled eggs and dead penguin chicks. During the first half of January, when the skua chicks are a few days old, and the penguin chicks almost

Figure 31   South Polar skua carries away an Adélie penguin egg.

Figure 32   The scavenging activity of South Polar skuas differs between edge and center of the Adélie penguin rookery at Cape Crozier: In early January the feeding territories of the skuas at the rookery edge contain chick carcasses with only the stomachs opened (top row), while in the remainder of the rookery all edible items have been consumed, and only the inedible bones of the pelvic girdle, remain.

four weeks, there may be many abandoned eggs (Fig. 31) and up to ten dead chicks in a feeding territory. At the same time, there are no consumable items left in the remaining parts of the rookery, i.e. in the center and beach areas. The skuas have cleaned up everything, and only bones lie on the ground (Fig. 32). There never remains an edible item: as soon as an egg or chick becomes available, it is spotted and picked up by the skuas, and the competition for this food is intense. Up to 15 skuas will compete for one penguin egg or chick, while in the feeding territories only one or two skuas—the territorial pair—respond to such a food item. Moreover, systematic experiments with feeding stations at different locations in the rookery showed that it takes 45 seconds on the average for skuas to discover a new food item in the "free-for-all" areas (center and beach) while in the feeding territories it takes over 11 minutes. There are always hungry skuas on the lookout in the open areas, while the pairs with feeding territories are saturated with food at the same time. Since most skuas at Cape Crozier were banded, we know that the skuas that hunt in the center and beach zones are either non-breeding bachelors or those that breed on the slopes above the penguin rookery and are without feeding territories of their own. Later in the season, in late January and early February, the owners of feeding territories consume all addled eggs and penguin chick carcasses and clean up the area. Thus, these skuas "manage" their resources: they defend them in times of surplus, even though they are not hungry, and can fall back on them later when no new eggs or chicks are available. Since the combined predation and scavenging pressure is lower than the feeding territories than in the "open-for-all" sections of the rookery, the Adélies breeding in the feeding territories of the skuas may actually derive a benefit from being "owned" by skuas. Thus, the peripheral zone of a large Adélie rookery may provide breeding advantages for both species and may approach a symbiotic relationship (Müller-Schwarze and Müller-Schwarze 1973).

In summary, the breeding South Polar skuas obtain their diet from the ocean as well as the from the Adélie rookeries. But they clearly prefer the terrestrial food source. Before they go fishing at sea, they may even eat pellets of penguin feathers and bones that had been regurgitated by other skuas as indigestible. Moreover, we found clean bones in the crops of skua chicks that had starved to death. This indicates that even starving skuas are reluctant to go to sea for food. During the frequent severe storms it is inconvenient to fish, and one can see skuas return from the ocean with ice-encrusted heads from dipping them into the water while sitting on ice floes. Thus, during blizzards the rookery is a convenient source of food. Skuas will not fly out at wind speeds of 40 miles per hour or more, and these are quite frequent. At Cape Crozier we recorded wind speeds exceeding 120 miles per hour.

Whether there are specialists among the skuas that are unable to switch to an alternative food source, is not known. Since penguin eggs and chicks are available for only 3 out of 12 months, skuas have to obtain their food from the surface of the ocean for most of the year in any case. The seasonal diet changes are reflected in the anatomy and behavior of the South Polar skua. The structure of bill and foot is a compromise between seabird and bird of prey. The bill is just large enough to carry a penguin egg and powerful enough to peck open an egg, but is not used for killing a penguin chick by aiming at head or neck. The South Polar skua does not possess an efficient killing movement in its behavioral repertoire. Instead, penguin chicks are literally eaten alive. First, a skua will pull a chick by its bill away from other penguins (adult as well as chicks) and into a neutral area. Then the skua tries to step onto the back of the chick and pecks on its head from behind. The eyes as the softest parts are pecked at first. If both partners of a skua pair have attacked and overwhelmed a penguin chick, one starts to eat at the head, while the other pecks at the cloaca and opens up the chick from behind. The chick is then still alive and utters distress calls. Compared to birds of prey or carnivorous mammals, this is an extremely unspecialized and inefficient way of catching and killing prey.

Within a population of South Polar skuas there are some specialists that have developed individual techniques of preying on penguins. We observed one skua among the 2000 at Cape Crozier that approached incubating penguins from behind and pulled them at their tail. The attacked penguin would defend itself by reaching over his shoulder and pecking at the skua. At the same time the standing penguin rocked and turned around his long axis. Sooner or later an egg would be visible behind or beside the penguin. That was the moment the skua had waited for: it quickly grabbed the egg with its beak (Fig. 31) and walked or flew to a point where it could open and eat it in peace.

Another skua fluttered into the dense crèches of Adélie chicks and disturbed the birds enough that the crèche divided into two groups. Single chicks of the smaller group then tried to run over to the main crèche. It was these isolated chicks that the skua attacked, most of the time successfully, while chicks in crèches usually are not attacked by skuas.

These examples show that single individuals may develop new behavior patterns with which to circumvent the otherwise very effective antipredator defenses of the prey species: Whether or not other skuas will copy these "innovations", or whether behavior will even spread through the skua population, remains to be seen.

The penguin mortality inflicted by the skuas is difficult to determine, since many eggs and chicks are carrion or at least dying at the time they are taken as food. Earlier estimates of 10 to 20% (Maher 1966) appear too high. The Adélies at Cape Royds, for instance, lay 1.81 eggs per nest, on the average, and raise 1.03 chicks successfully (Taylor 1962). Thus the loss amounts to 43% and regardless of how these eggs and chicks die, they all end up as skua food, alive or dead.

We have determined the food consumption of pairs of South Polar skuas in a series of feeding experiments. After placing abundant addled eggs or dead penguin chicks near a skua nest, we recorded how much was consumed every 24 hours. A pair of skuas ate 11 eggs per day on the average. If all 2000 skuas at Cape Crozier ate at that rate, 477,000 eggs would be removed during the 45 days that eggs are available. As for the consumption of penguin chicks, a pair of skuas ate 950 grams per day. Again, 2000 skuas could eat 51,000 kg meat during the chick season of approximately 50 days. This is equivalent to 114,000 penguin chicks, taking into account their growth curve. Eggs and chicks taken together, a total of 591,000 individuals could be removed if all skuas fed on penguins all the time, and the penguins' defenses were ineffective. This would be more than 3 times the number of eggs that are laid originally, obviously an impossibility. This estimate, crude by necessity, shows that the skuas at Cape Crozier could never obtain all their food from the rookery. Instead only about one-eighth of their calculated food requirements comes from the rookery. The penguins' anti-predator defenses make it very difficult for the skuas to hunt in the rookery.

## ANTI-PREDATOR BEHAVIOR

The anti-predator behavior of Adélie penguins is aimed primarily at the leopard seal in the water and the South Polar skua in the penguin rookery.

*Behavior vis-à-vis leopard seal*

In their interactions with the leopard seal, Adélie penguins may reduce the chance of an encounter (predator avoidance), or may increase their distance after an encounter (flight behavior).

*Predator Avoidance.* About six behavior patterns are in the service of avoiding the leopard seal.

a) Adélie penguins enter the water only if absolutely necessary, for instance to forage, migrate, or commute between rookery and fishing grounds. Whenever possible, they stay on ice floes, also using them as rafts. Instead of swimming 50 or 100 m from an ice floe to the beach, they often wait many hours until the floe has drifted ashore and they can leap onto solid ground. If there is a row of ice floes at an angle to their intended direction, they walk from floe to floe as far as possible even if it temporarily deflects them from their direction of travel.

b) Walking on fast ice, Adélies prefer the thick ice and the higher parts of the ice, since the leopard seal can easily push through the ice from below. At the edge of a patch of thin ice the group's movement comes to a halt, and only after lengthy hesitation do single penguins hurry over the treacherous surface.

c) Hydrophone recordings show that penguins returning from a foraging trip do not vocalize under water. They only vocalize when close to shore and exchanging signals with Adélies waiting at the beach.

d) The swimming style of "porpoising" makes it difficult for an aquatic predator to zero in on a particular individual. The re-entry point of a porpoising penguin cannot be predicted from launch data available to a predator in the water, and the momentarily airborne penguin is invisible to a predator underwater and cannot be heard easily (Hui, 1981).

e) Adélies, when gathered at the beach for departure, observe returning groups. Only when large groups, i.e. with more than 25 penguins, return undisturbed to the beach, will those waiting at the beach walk or jump into the water. They leave after an exchange of vocalizations. Thirty-one percent of the returning groups with 26–30 members triggered departure in waiting penguins, while small groups with 1–5 Adélies did so only in 11% of the cases. Single penguins or small groups may be dispersed members of a larger group that has been attacked by the leopard seal.

f) A single penguin is more alert than one in a group. In our observations, Adélies standing by themselves turned their heads 11 times per minute, while those in groups do this only 6 times per minute.

*Flight behavior* includes the following behavior patterns:

a) If the leopard seal charges through thin ice from below, the penguins escape on foot into different directions. A single, isolated penguin will stand motionless, sometimes for hours. We observed one Adélie which remained motionless for 80 minutes after such an attack, until his ice floe touched another on which a large group of penguins was standing. He then walked across and joined the other group.

b) Upon being attacked by a leopard seal under water, a group of Adélies flees in many different directions. They gather again after about 30–40 seconds.

c) Groups of swimming penguins that come near a leopard seal, change their direction, often abruptly, and dive for a period longer than normal (13 seconds on the average), instead of continuing to "porpoise", when they emerge every five seconds. After an attack their rhythm accelerates, so that they emerge every four seconds.

d) On ice floes Adélies approach a resting leopard seal to about three meters (Fig. 33). Even other seals that pose no danger to penguins, such as Weddell seals, are not approached any closer (Fig. 34). Only chicks do not respect this "safe" distance. They peck sleeping Weddell seals on the nose, or even climb on their backs, as they would do on an ice block. Just as they do on land with Weddell seals, the chicks don't show any avoidance or escape behavior when encountering the leopard seal in the water.

*Behavior vis-à-vis South Polar Skua*

The Adélies have to defend their eggs and chicks against skuas (adult

Figure 33    Adélie penguins on an ice floe keep a distance of at least 3 m from a resting leopard seal.

Figure 34   At the beach, Adélie penguins keep the same distance from a (non-dangerous) Weddell seal as they do from a leopard seal. Only chicks approach a seal closely.

penguins are themselves not threatened). The anti-predator behavior against skuas varies with the distance and behavior of the skua. Flying skuas are ignored, as long as they are 14 m or higher above ground. Lower flying birds are observed by the penguins and at flight altitudes of 50 cm or lower the Adélies attack the skuas with open bills and raucous vocalizations. Skuas that stand or walk close to penguin colonies, are attacked and chased away by relieved breeding birds or non-breeding bachelors (Fig. 35).

We conducted experiments with two-dimensional geometric figures and "skuas" that were moved over penguin groups. The larger the dummy was, the stronger the response by the penguins, but the shape of the silhouette did not play a role. In the penguin rookeries of the Antarctic continent there is usually just one large flying bird species, the South Polar skua. Hence, every overflight means potential danger, and the penguins don't need to finely discriminate shapes of flying birds, as waterfowl in temperate latitudes do. There, many different species fly about, among them birds of prey. Our dummy experiments extended over the entire breeding season. We found that the interspecific aggression of the penguins against the skuas is greatest in mid-December, the time the Adélie chicks hatch. The penguins are thus most defensive when their chicks are most vulnerable (Müller-Schwarze and Müller-Schwarze 1977).

Chicks respond to skuas at the age of two to three weeks, the time when they gather in crèches. Once a skua has attacked a chick, it is most often the adult that chases away the skua (8 times in 11 observed cases). The typical reaction of crèched chicks to attacking skuas is dodging, moving away, and concentrating in a tight cluster. This also occurred in response to skua dummies overhead. Like the adults, the larger the dummy was, the more vigorously the chicks responded. Tight huddles are also formed when humans approach too close to a crèche.

## DIET AND FORAGING

All seabirds and seals that breed or live on the Antarctic continent and its islands obtain their food from the ocean. One of these species is the Adélie penguin, which enters the water for foraging and for bathing. During the breeding season there is a steady stream of Adélies on their way to and from the ocean to carry food to their young. The collected food is transported in the proventriculus, which is located low in the body, and is regurgitated at the nest. To feed the young, the bill is opened, and the chick reaches deep into the parent's bill with its own. It picks up the food that is semi-digested and mixed with a "crop secretion." The bill positions during feeding are the reverse of that in passerine birds, where the parent's bill is inserted into the gaping mouth of the nestlings. Depositing food into the nest, as in birds of prey, gulls or terns, would not be possible because there are constantly skuas or sheathbills looking for food, and they would pick up the dropped food, or even actively interfere with the

Figure 35    Adult Adélie penguins chasing a South Polar skua.

feeding. This interference results in larger amounts of food dropped on the ground that is lost for the penguins, but will be gobbled up greedily by the scavenger/predators.

The food that Adélie penguins bring from the ocean to their nests has been analyzed by pumping up the stomach contents. Emison (1968) found at Cape Crozier that the most frequent organism in the proventriculus of Adélies was a small crustacean, *Euphausia crystallorophias*, and a little schooling fish, *Pleuragramma antarcticum*. *Euphausia superba* was rarer in the penguins' diet. In addition there were 2 fish species of the family *Chaenichthyidae* and 14 species of amphipods. According to numbers of individuals found in the stomach, euphausiids were most frequent (91–95%), followed by fish (4–8%), and amphipods (less than 2%). By volume there were 60% euphausiids, 39% fish, and 1% amphipods. In this context it should be remembered that the euphausiids are the "krill" that represents the main diet of the large baleen whales. Since the whales have been decimated so severely, it has been suggested that additional krill for about 300 million more penguins is available. Thus far, only the chinstrap penguin has increased in numbers. For instance, the chinstrap rookery at Entrance Point at Deception Island has increased 10 fold in 25 years (Müller-Schwarze and Todd unpubl.).

## THERMOREGULATION

Its dense plumage and thick layer of blubber insulate the Adélie penguin very effectively against the ambient temperatures. Heat loss can be dramatic in the Antarctic, both in the supercooled water (up to $-1.6°$ C, or $29.2°$ F in Ross Sea) and the cold air on land. The chilling effect depends not only on the air temperature, but even more so on the wind speeds. The chill factor can be calculated from both temperature and wind speed, and is expressed as calories (lost) per hour and square meter surface. However, for the Adélie penguin it is a greater problem to dissipate heat during sunshine or exertion than to conserve heat in the cold. Adélies lose heat through their flippers, feet and open beaks. When the ambient temperature rises above the freezing point, adults, but even more so chicks, start to pant with bills open and tongues exposed. On particular "hot" days the chicks lie flat on the ground, belly down. The feet are stretched out, with the underside up.

The body temperature of adult Adélies varies between $37.7°$ and $40.2°$ C as determined by Goldsmith and Sladen (1961) with a thermoelement inserted into the stomach. Similar values ($37.7°$ to $39.6°$ C) were measured with a thermistor implanted into the abdominal cavity (Sladen et al. 1966). During the first 8 days the chicks cannot regulate their body temperature themselves and are dependent on their parents for thermal protection (Sapin-Jaloustre 1960). At about 9 days of age they start to regulate their body temperature themselves, and by the time they are 15 days old temperature regulation functions as well in them as in adult birds. Chicks are able to live independently outside the nest at the age of 15 days. As long as they wear their down plumage, they are unable to maintain their body temperature when in the water.

The temperature in the interior of an Adélie egg is 33.7° C, before the embryo itself produces heat. This is about 6.6° C less than the body temperature of the adult bird. The temperature inside the egg was measured with the aid of a small transmitter implanted under the egg shell (Eklund and Charlton 1959). At Sea World, San Diego, an incubation temperature of 96.5° F was measured with biotelemetry (Todd pers. comm.).

## MOLT

The molt of the Adélie penguin has been investigated by Cendron (1953), Sapin-Jaloustre (1960), Penney (1967), Mougin (1968) and others.

The chicks molt twice. Their down plumage at hatching is silver-gray with an almost black head. Gradually, as the chick grows, new down grows in, until the second, anthracite-colored plumage is completed at the age of three weeks when the chicks start to gather in crèches. Finally, when they are 8 weeks old, the chicks molt into the waterproof feather coat with bluish-black back and white abdomen and throat.

Like many other birds, the adult Adélies molt only once a year. This occurs after the end of the breeding season. The molt starts around February 15th and lasts 3 weeks. The birds stay on land, or on ice floes during that time. The peak of the molt occurs in the first week of March, and with the beginning of April all penguins have left the rookery. Penney (1967) distinguishes eight stages of the molt, grouped into three pre-molt and four molt stages, followed by the eighth, the post-molt.

During the first pre-molt stage the birds come ashore and proceed to wind-protected snow slopes. They are fat, their plumage appears dull, and the feathers on their backs have brown tips. The flippers swell during the second stage. The scale feathers lose their sheen and the contour feathers still remain in place. The flippers swell to twice their normal thickness during the third pre-molt stage. The body feathers are erected so that the bird appears larger than usual. The flippers are supplied with so much blood that they often start to bleed when hitting a rock or an ice block.

The molt proper starts with the shedding of feathers on the middle of the back and the middle of the abdomen (first molt stage). The new feathers push out the old. During the second molt stage one-fourth of all new feathers in the abdominal region are visible, and at stage three half of all new features are visible on abdomen, chin, cheeks, rump, tail, and on the leading edge and the tips of the flippers (Fig. 36). Finally, three quarters of all new features are visible during the fourth stage. Bunches

Figure 36   Molting adult Adélie penguin (stage 3–4) on the left; at right a chick.

of old feathers are still in place on the front of the neck, top of the head, and on the sides of neck and legs.

During the post-molt the Adélies appear thin, and in some individuals the sternum is visible under the skin. The new dark feathers on head, chin, and back have blue tips, and the tail is still short.

Since they must fast Adélie penguins lose 40–50% of their body weight while completing their molt. Drastic weight losses during the molt are typical for all penguins. King penguins for instance, lose 0.2 to 0.3 kg daily during their molt, which lasts 32 days. Their weight drops from 20 to 11 kg (Stonehouse 1960). Molting penguins (several species examined) use twice as much energy as required for basal metabolism only.

By comparison, incubation requires 1.3 to 1.4 times the estimated cost of basal metabolism (Croxall 1982).

The rectal temperature of Adélie penguins rises by 1° C during the molt. With this increased metabolism, behavioral thermoregulation becomes particularly important. Molting birds stay at protected places where the air temperature may be 2.5° C higher than the temperature of the general area, and the wind speed may be only one-fifth of that prevailing in unprotected areas (Mougin 1968).

# Chapter 2

## THE CHINSTRAP PENGUIN___

Compared to the Adélie penguin, the breeding cycle and behavior of the chinstrap penguin has been little investigated, although it is a fascinating, and perhaps in certain ways a key penguin species. The chinstrap is restricted to a small longitudinal sector, and it is the closest relative of the extremely Antarctic Adélie penguin. The author has worked with chinstrap penguins in the South Shetlands (Nelson and King George Islands). Chinstraps prefer steep, rocky or boulder strewn slopes (Fig. 37), while Adélies and gentoo penguins settle on more level ground, if it is available (Figs. 6 and 46).

### PHYSICAL FEATURES

The chinstrap is about 67 cm long; the back, top of the head, upperside of flippers, and tail are black. The species name is derived from the thin black stripe that runs from the occiput, below the eye and under the throat to the other side of the head, so that the bird appears to be wearing a helmet (Fig. 38). The bill is black and slightly longer (6.6 cm) than in the Adélie penguin.

Cheeks, chin, throat, breast and abdomen are white. The underside of the flipper is white, except for a black blotch on the proximal half of

95

Figure 37   Chinstrap penguins breed on steep boulder-strewn slopes and hills. Nelson Island, South Shetland Islands.

Figure 38    Head of Chinstrap penguin.

the flipper. The inside of the bill and the tongue are whitish, the feet are pink to yellowish with brown toenails, and the cloaca is black.

The chicks of the chinstrap hatch with a white to silver-gray down coat. The underside of the flippers is of the same color. Eyes and bill are black already, feet and cloaca are pink. The toenails are ivory colored and brown only at the tips.

When about 2 weeks old, head and back of the chicks change to slate grey, while the ventral side from chin to abdomen changes to a light gray. Thus, a clear contrast exists between the dark back and the lighter belly. The black stripe under the chin is already visible in chicks of the crèche stage. The second molt at the end of the crèche phase results in the final, waterproof plumage.

## BREEDING BIOLOGY

The breeding cycle of the chinstrap has been investigated by Bagshawe (1938), Sladen (1955), Conroy et al. (1974), Trivelpiece and Volkman (1979), and Volkman et al. (1980). Chinstrap penguins breed 3–4 weeks later than Adélies in the same area. On Signy Island in the South Orkney Islands the 2 eggs were laid around December 1, and the chicks hatched

Figure 39    Ecstatic Display of a chinstrap penguin. Note its chick in the guard stage.

in the first week of January. The egg-laying and hatching dates for the Adélie were November 10 and December 15, respectively.

According to Conroy et al. (1974) the chinstraps arrive on Signy Island (60° 43′S, 45° 38′W) during the first week of November and start building nests immediately. Egg-laying peaked around November 25. The date of egg-laying varies with the geographical latitude. Further to the north, on South Georgia (54° 15′S, 36° 45′W) clutches have been found in October (Carcelles 1931), while at Waterboat Point (64° 49′S, 62° 52′W) eggs were laid during the first week of December (Bagshawe 1938). On King George Island the dates are essentially the same (Trivelpiece and Volkman 1980). The eggs are incubated for 35 to 37 days and at Waterboat Point the chicks hatched during the first half of January.

The behavior of the chinstrap during pair formation and raising of the young resembles very much that of the Adélie penguin. The "ecstatic" display (Fig. 39), loud and quiet mutual displays (Fig. 40) differ in their

Figure 40   Mutual Display in a breeding pair of chinstrap penguins. The bird on the right utters a Loud Mutual Display (open bill), the left bird has bill almost closed in a Quiet Mutual Display.

form only slightly from those of the Adélie penguin. When relieving each other at the nest, the arriving mate walks around the nest in exaggerated steps, while nodding his head up and down. The intensity of this "pompous gait" or "circling" is indicative of the pair's readiness to "change the guard" (Müller-Schwarze and Müller-Schwarze 1980).

The nests of the chinstrap are less elaborate than those of Adélie or gentoo penguins. Sometimes a nest consists of only 8 or 10 pebbles, just enough to prevent the eggs from rolling off a ledge. The clutch consists of 2 (1–3) eggs (Fig. 41). During egg-laying, many males go to sea and will return only after 10 days. Therefore, the females incubate for the first few days and fast for a total of 30 days. During the five weeks of incubation the mates relieve each other more often than the Adélie penguin does. One parent stays on the nest for only 2–3 days at a time (Figs. 42–44).

Very few eggs are lost. In the study by Conroy et al. (1974) 90% of the eggs hatched, and 84% of the chicks survived until fledging. This is

Figure 41    Chinstrap penguin on the nest with 2 eggs.

75% of all laid eggs. This is a breeding success of 1.83 chicks per pair, considerably higher than for instance that of Adélie penguins in the Ross Sea. Predators in the rookery are skuas and sheathbills (Fig. 45). In late February and early March only a few adults remain in the rookery. In early March the chinstraps return to the beaches in order to molt. The molt lasts about two weeks. In contrast to the Adélie penguin, many chinstraps stay longer in the colony, show signs of pair formation, perform the "loud mutual" display, and are interested in nests. This is a consequence of the more favorable ice conditions, which permit the chinstraps to find food near their rookery for a longer time than would be possible for the Adélie penguin. The latter is forced to migrate north immediately after completion of breeding and molting.

   More detailed counts since the late 1950s have shown that the chinstrap penguin has increased in numbers. For instance, the chinstrap rookery at Entrance Point on Deception Island in the South Shetlands had 150

Figure 44   Chinstrap penguin feeding its young.

Figure 45   Sheathbill eats a Chinstrap clutch that had been exposed by a disturbance.

Figure 46   Chinstrap penguins breeding among Adélies, often after fighting and displacing established pairs of the other species.

Figure 47    Interspecific aggression: Gentoo defends nest against approaching Chinstrap. Nelson Island, South Shetland Islands.

nests in 1957, 350 in 1965, 450 in 1967 (Croxall 1978), and we counted 1464 chicks in January 1982. Using the figures given above for breeding success, there must have been over 1000 nests at the beginning of the 1981/82 season. Thus, in this rookery, the number of breeding pairs more than doubled in 14 years, and increased seven-fold in 24 years. The annual increase averaged about 10%.

Furthermore, arriving chinstrap penguins also fight with established Adélies and evict them successfully from their nests, as we observed in 1976 at Point Thomas, King George Island (Müller-Schwarze et al. 1977). There, several hundred pairs of chinstraps are involved in this annual battle between the species (Fig. 46). Recently the author also observed agonistic behavior between breeding gentoo penguins and approaching chinstraps on Nelson Island. The incubating gentoos successfully warded off the chinstraps by open-bill threats (Fig. 47). On Nelson Island, one whole gentoo colony of about 100 pairs has been displaced by chinstraps between 1971 and 1983.

# Chapter 3

# THE GENTOO PENGUIN_____

## PHYSICAL FEATURES

The adult gentoo penguin is characterized by the white band ("bonnet") that extends across the top of the head from one eye to the other, and is narrower in the middle (Fig. 48). In addition, there are white speckles sprinkled over the head behind the white headband, particularly in the northern subspecies, such as the gentoos on the Falkland Islands. The bill is up to 8 cm long and orange-red, with a black upper edge to the upper mandible and a tiny dark black bill-tip. The tongue and lining of the mouth are intensely orange-red.

The gentoo is larger than the Adélie or chinstrap penguins and measures 70–80 cm in length. Back, upper side of flipper, occiput, forehead, throat and tail are black. Breast, abdomen, the underside of the flipper and a ring around the eye are white. The feet are orange-red, with black toenails.

The chicks of the gentoo penguin are primarily dark grey on the head, the nape of the neck, and on the back and upper side of the flipper. Abdomen, throat and underside of the flipper are white. The flippers droop loosely from the body, and there is more white visible at the edge of the flipper in the chick than there is in the adult. The feet and sides of the bill are red; the underside of the bill is only partially red, the rest is covered

Figure 48   Gentoo penguin with 2 chicks on the nest during the guard stage.

with white feathers. The white head band that is so characteristic of adults can be seen in the chick only as a fine line in the dark grey down on the top of the head. The non-breeding younger gentoos are similar to the adults, but chin and throat are not yet black as in adults. The black plumage is sprinkled with white; they appear as if dusted with flour. Often the white eye ring is also still missing.

## BREEDING BIOLOGY

Both subspecies of the gentoo penguin have not been investigated as intensively as this fascinating species would warrant. We owe our knowledge of the basic breeding cycle and behavior of the gentoo above all to Bagshawe (1938), Roberts (1940), Gwynn (1953a), Zinderen Bakker (1971), and Williams (1980).

Bagshawe (1938) studied gentoo penguins at Waterboat Point (64° 49'S, 62° 52'W) in the area of the Antarctic Peninsula during the years 1921 and 1922. He estimated the number of birds in the colony at over 12,000. On December 28, 1980 only 540 gentoo nests were left at Waterboat Point (author's own observation). A station has displaced most of the penguins. In Bagshawe's study, the gentoos appeared as early as August in the rookery, and by September 18 thousands had arrived. Many came in pairs, and displayed courtship behavior. Bagshawe concluded from this that gentoo arrive paired in the rookery, quite in contrast to Adélie penguins. Copulations occur from October through December, and nest building is typical for the month of November. The nests are large (Fig. 49). Bagshawe counted 1700 pebbles and 70 old tail feathers in one nest of medium size. The clutch consists of 2 eggs (Fig. 50), but we have repeatedly found nests with 4 eggs, possibly from 2 different females. The second egg is laid 3 days after the first, and incubation starts about 24 hours before laying the second egg, and lasts for 35 days. Egg-laying in a gentoo rookery is not as well synchronized as in other penguin species (Gwynn 1953a). On Heard Island (53° 06'S, 73° 30'E) the first egg was laid on October 26, and a part of the rookery had complete clutches on November 7. The time of egg-laying depends on the snow cover. On Macquarie Island (54° 30'S, 159° E) snow does not play an important role, and gentoos lay their eggs more than six weeks earlier than on Heard Island. With increasing southern latitude the eggs are laid later, from early June on Marion Island (47° S, 38° E) to late November in the Antarctic. On Heard Island the gentoo chicks hatch in mid-December while—according to Bagshawe—they hatched only in early and mid-January further south at Waterboat Point. When incubating, the mates relieve each other every 24 hours. The temperature of the incubated egg is 28° C on the average (Zinderen Bakker 1971).

The behavior of the northern race of the gentoo penguin has been studied by Zinderen Bakker on Prince Edward and Marion Islands, located

Figure 49    Gentoo penguin on his nest, built between whale bones for wind protection. Port Lockroy, Antarctic Peninsula.

Figure 50   At the southern end of its range the Gentoo penguin builds his nest from pebbles and tail feathers of penguins. The typical clutch consists of 2 eggs.

almost halfway between Africa and Antarctica. There the gentoos stay in or near the rookery all year round (as they do in the Falkland Islands). During the breeding season there are three classes of birds that differ in their behavior: breeders, unsuccessful breeders, and non-breeders.

The two main displays of the gentoo penguin are the "trumpet call" and the "bow-gape-hiss." The trumpet call is the equivalent of the ecstatic and mutual displays of other penguins and sounds like the braying of a donkey ("ee-haw"). It is uttered with the head pointing skyward, and the bill is wide open (Fig. 51), revealing the bright red inner lining of the mouth. Males perform it by themselves on their territories; thus, contextually, if not functionally, it resembles the ecstatic display of Adélie and chinstrap penguins. The trumpet call can also be uttered by the two mates simultaneously, i.e. as a loud mutual display. The main difference between the gentoo's loud mutual display and that of the other pygoscelids is that the gentoo stretches his neck up, but does not wave the head sideways. In the "bow-gape-hiss" a bird bends down with the tip of the bill almost touching the ground, and opens his bill so that the red lining is visible (Fig. 52). While opening the bill, a single hissing sound is uttered. The mate may or may not join in. Whenever a gentoo deposits a pebble at the nest, he hisses when opening the bill to release the pebble. Therefore, we consider the "bow-gape-hiss" a display that is derived from nest-building. The frequency of the "bow-gape-hiss" upon return of a mate is indicative of the time of nest relief; the more joint displays the sooner the birds will relieve each other (Müller-Schwarze and Müller-Schwarze 1980).

The male starts to build the nest and displays at the nest with the loud trumpeting. After a female has joined him, he carries nest material and the female builds it into the nest. The nest material varies from pebbles and a few molted penguin tail feathers in Antarctica (Fig. 50) to a stone base covered with humus and plant material in South Georgia, to completely plant matter on Heard, Marion, and Prince-Edward Islands.

The chicks hatch at an interval of 24 hours and are dark grey. When one week old, the second, lighter down coat starts to grow. In contrast to Adélie and chinstrap chicks, the gentoo penguin chick has a light ventral side and a dark back (Fig. 53) from the time of hatching. The chick remains in the nest until its fifth week. After that the chicks gather in crèches (Fig. 54). Since the chicks hatch on different days, they are different in size, and in many cases only the larger one survives. In Zinderen Bakker's study 11 out of 20 chicks survived until their fifth week, when the crèches started to form.

Predators of gentoo penguins are birds that usually forage at sea or feed on carrion, but will take sick penguins, eggs, or small chicks when available. These are the southern and northern giant petrel (*Macronectes giganteus* and *M. halli*), brown skua (*Catharacta skua*), Dominican gull (*Larus dominicanus*), and sheathbill (*Chionis alba* and *minor*; Fig. 45).

Figure 51   Loud Mutual Display of the Gentoo penguin. The bright red lining of the mouth is visible, and a donkey call is uttered. Note that the chick is participating in the display.

Figure 52   "Bow-gape-hiss" of the Gentoo penguin. It typically occurs during nest-relief.

Figure 53   Gentoo penguin feeding its chicks. Nelson Island, South Shetlands.

Figure 54   Gentoo chicks lie flat on the ground in a storm.

# Chapter 4

# THE EMPEROR PENGUIN___

## PHYSICAL FEATURES

The emperor penguin is the largest of all penguins (Fig. 55). It stands up to 112 cm high and weighs about 30 kg. Head, back and tail are bluish-black, the beak is purple on its sides, and the sides of the neck and throat are yellow to orange, but never as colorful as those of the king penguin. The front from chest to the feathers of the feet is shiny white with a faint yellow hue. The emperor penguin is distinguished from the king penguin by its larger size, smaller, feathered feet, and paler yellow on the throat. In the emperor the neck is dark only at the sides, while in the king penguin the dark plumage of the back comes forward in two corners that almost meet at the throat.

## HISTORY OF DISCOVERY

The emperor penguin, as the largest and most perfectly cold-adapted polar bird, which breeds on sea ice and can fast for over four months, has always been particularly fascinating to Antarctic explorers.

The emperor penguin, *Aptenodytes forsteri*, was named after the two German naturalists G. and J. R. Forster, father and son, who accompanied James Cook on his circumnavigation of the world in 1772–1775. They

Figure 55    Size difference between Emperor (right) and Adélie penguins. Cape Crozier.

described the king penguin, but Gray (1844) assumed that their illustrations depicted an emperor penguin. Neither Cook nor the Forsters ever reported an Antarctic penguin the size of an emperor, although they reached the pack ice repeatedly. Because of this uncertainty, we now consider Thaddeus von Bellingshausen as the discoverer of the emperor penguin. He caught one specimen in December 1820. G. R. Gray then described the emperor penguin in 1844, using specimens brought back by James Clark Ross' expedition in 1839–1843.

The first breeding colony was found during the first Scott expedition on the ship *Discovery*. In October 1902 the expedition member R. S. Skelton discovered the emperor penguin rookery at Cape Crozier. A month later C. W. R. Royds of the same expedition visited the rookery to collect material. But the penguins had left their colony, and Royds found only 1 frozen egg.

From these observations it became obvious that the emperor penguin does not breed during the summer, as do the Adélies in the same area. They had to follow a different annual rhythm. Therefore, Edward A. Wilson, zoologist, physician, and artist on both Scott expeditions, visited Cape Crozier in mid-winter during the second ("Terra Nova") expedition. Wilson, H. R. Bowers, and Apsley Cherry-Garrard traveled the 70 miles from Cape Evans to Cape Crozier in the storms and darkness of the polar night, man-hauling their sleds. They collected 3 eggs for embryological studies. Temperatures reached -60.8° C. This experience has been described by Cherry-Garrard in his 1922 book "The worst journey in the world".

The second emperor penguin rookery was discovered at Haswell Island (60° 31'S, 93° 00'E) in 1912 by the Australian expedition led by Sir Douglas Mawson. This is the same year that Wilson and Scott perished together on their way back from the South Pole.

It was not until 1948 that the third emperor rookery was found. It is located on solid land on Dion Island (67° 52'S, 68° 43'W) and was described by B. Stonehouse. The next colony was discovered in 1950 at Pointe Géologie (66° 40'S, 140° 01'E) in Adélie Land (Sapin-Jaloustre 1952). Today we know over 30 rookeries around the Antarctic continent. Budd (1961) described and compared those that were known until 1960. The largest one numbers 100,000 birds and is located on the west side of Coulman Island (73° 28'S, 149° 05'E). On November 9, 1964 I visited an emperor rookery at Cape Roget (71° 59'S, 170° 31'E) in Victorialand with the first group of people that had ever set foot on that breeding site. The day before a helicopter pilot had seen the breeding birds from the air. With about 40,000 birds this is the second largest known emperor penguin rookery (Fig. 56).

## BREEDING BIOLOGY

The breeding biology and behavior of the emperor penguin has been

Figure 56  Emperor penguins in their breeding colony on the fast ice at Cape Roget, Ross Sea.

elucidated by Stonehouse (1952, 1953) and Prévost (1961). Stonehouse worked in the colony of Dion Island, which numbers just under 300 birds, while Prévost had 12,500 emperor penguins in his rookery. Because of the larger sample sizes, the following account is based primarily on Prévost's data.

Breeding takes place on the fast ice where the emperors spend ten months every year. They arrive at the breeding site in March. The most important behavior patterns during pair formation are the "courtship song with bowing" (Fr.: "chant") and "standing opposite with sky pointing" (Fr.: "parade mutuelle"). The search for a mate lasts several hours to a few days, and copulations occur from mid-April to early June. They are particularly frequent between April 20 and 25. The pair bond is lasting: during one breeding season only five of 73 banded pairs separated. The egg, which weighs 450 grams, is laid between May 1 and June 12. The dates of laying the colony's first egg varied by only 8 days in 16 years of observation (Guillottin and Jouventin 1979). When the female lays the egg, the male utters the "courtship song" and the female often joins in. Before the female passes the egg to the male for incubation, both display with "parade mutuelle" and "chant". The male rolls the egg on his foot and covers it with his abdominal flap. Then the female leaves for the sea to feed. Almost all females leave the rookery in May. By then they have fasted for one and a half months. During that time they have lost 17–38% of their body weight.

Incubation starts in May, and some birds still have eggs in August. The mean temperature of the brooded egg is 34.4° C. During incubation emperor penguins gather in large huddles, called "tortues" (turtles) by Prévost. This behavior is an important form of social thermoregulation in the extreme Antarctic winter with its darkness, an average temperature of -20.3° C and wind speeds of 9.9 meters per second, on the average. Incubation lasts 62–66 days, and females start to return in late June, when the first eggs hatch. Then the male has incubated continuously for two months. From the time of his arrival in the rookery until the female's return, the male has fasted for up to four and a half months. During this time he may lose more than 10 kg, which is up to 50% of his body weight.

The chicks hatch in July. Initially, they are almost naked from the neck down. This facilitates heat transfer from the parent bird. Only the head is feathered. It will protrude from the brood flap. First, the female feeds and broods the chick, while the male feeds at sea. Later the parents take turns. The chicks spend about one and a half months in the brood pouch of the parents, and from early September to December they live in crèches (Fig. 57). Parents recognize their chicks by voice; the chick-specific song is present at hatching and does not change for 5 months. This is in contrast to the Adélie penguin where the chick-specific song develops after 10 days of age (Jouventin 1982). The chicks have molted to their seaworthy

Figure 57   Emperor penguins in their breeding colony at Cape Crozier, Ross Island. The chicks are 3–4 months old. In the foreground a chick pecks at a South Polar skua.

Figure 58   Chick mortality in the Emperor penguin: a snowstorm killed hundreds of chicks in the colony at Beaufort Island. Photo: Frank S. Todd.

plumage when the fast ice breaks up in December. They now ride the ice floes into the sea. If the ice breaks up early, when the chicks still have their down coat, they will be soaked by spray and waves. Then mortality may reach 100%. Mortality due to storms can also be high when the chicks are still in the rookery (Jouventin 1975; Todd 1980; Fig. 58). Emperor penguins are sexually mature at 4–8 years (average 5.8 years for males, 5 for females; Guillottin and Jouventin 1979).

The main predators of the emperor penguin are the leopard seal and the killer whale. The emperor penguin's diet consists of squid and fish. It can dive to at least 265 m depth (Kooyman et al. 1971).

# Chapter 5

# THE KING PENGUIN _____

The king penguin (Fig. 59) is somewhat familiar to many zoo visitors. Zoos keep it because of its great show value. It breeds on subantarctic islands, such as the Falklands, South Georgia, Marion Island, Kerguelen, Macquarie and Heard Islands. In the past, large numbers of king penguins were killed for their oil.

## PHYSICAL FEATURES

The king is smaller than the emperor, is less feathered on bill and feet, the dark plumage of the back reaches further toward to the throat, and the lateral neck patches are a brilliant orange in contrast to the paler color of the emperor.

## BREEDING BIOLOGY

A king penguin colony of 4000 birds on South Georgia in the southern Atlantic Ocean has provided astonishing information on the breeding biology of this unusual bird (Stonehouse 1960).

On South Georgia there are five king penguin colonies, all on beach terraces (Fig. 60). Typically, the colonies extend and expand from the beach up the slopes and are surrounded by tussock grass (*Poa flabellata*).

Figure 59    King penguin, incubating an egg.

Figure 60  King penguin rookery at Salisbury Plains, South Georgia. Year-old chicks and adults incubating eggs can be seen simultaneously.

However, a small rookery in Hope Valley at Elsehul on South Georgia is inland. The greatest surprise was that Stonehouse found the king penguin to breed only twice in three years. The raising of the young requires more than a year, about 13–14 months. Eggs are laid from late November through April. A pair that lays early in one season, fledges their chick in time to breed late the following year. This second chick, however, will fledge so late that the pair will not lay another egg that season. Instead, they will be ready early in the third season. Hence, 2 chicks are reared in 3 years. Because of this staggered type of breeding, eggs and fledging chicks can be seen at the same time in a rookery, and birds are occupied with breeding or raising young at all times of the year.

In May the weather deteriorates enough to stop all courtship and breeding attempts until September. Only feeding of the chicks continues. In January and February a king penguin rookery contains newly hatched chicks, incubating birds, one year old chicks (Fig. 60), courting pairs and molting individuals in all stages of the molt.

The annual cycle of the king penguin consists of molt (October), stay at sea (November), courtship (late November/early December), incubation (December and January), and rearing the young (February to December). On South Georgia the first eggs are laid in late November, while on the Kerguelen Islands, which are 5° further north, this occurs in October. Only the king penguin has such an extremely extended egg-laying period (late November through mid-April). By contrast, the gentoo penguins breeding on South Georgia lay only for a period of 2 months, and the extremely Antarctic Adélie penguin needs less than 1 month. The chicks of the king penguin that hatch late have slim survival chances, so that only about three months can be considered as a biologically meaningful egg-laying period.

The molt starts in September or October, lasts about 1 month, and is accompanied by a considerable weight loss. During that time the body weight drops from 20 to 12 kg. After the molt the king penguins go to sea (Fig. 61), forage and fatten up, before they come ashore to breed.

At the beginning of courtship the males stretch their heads to the almost vertical position and utter "short calls" and "long calls." These vocalizations attract females, but other males attack the caller. Likewise, a calling female is attacked by other females, but males walk over to her. When a pair is being formed, both birds stand opposite each other and face away with their bills ("head flagging"). Such initial bonding is often only temporary, and with the arrival of new birds new liaisons are formed all the time. The male repeatedly walks in front of the female in an "advertisement walk" ("waddling gait": Jouventin 1982), with his head turned alternately left and right. The female follows the male. Sometimes several females follow, and fights between them ensue. The role of the orange neck patches became obvious in an experiment: Stonehouse covered the

Figure 61    King penguins in the water. Lusitania Bay, Macquarie Island.

patches of two males with black paint. No female would follow these males during their "advertisement walk" as long as the colorful patches remained invisible.

The pair walk through the rookery, female behind male, until they have found a quiet place. With consolidation of the pair bond king penguins tend to stay at a particular site and engage in two displays that are typical for paired birds: "high-pointing" and "dabbling." During "high-pointing" both mates point their bills upward, and wave their heads slightly sideways, without uttering a sound. "Dabbling" is a lowering of the head, with the bill rapidly opening and closing, producing a rattling noise. During dabbling the penguin may also pick up a pebble. After the pair has spent 2–3 days at the same site, copulation occurs. Copulation is initiated when the male "dabbles" and rubs his bill on the female. After copulation, both mates "dabble" again. With the permanent pair formation completed, male and female utter frequently joint "long calls." The egg is laid 4–8 days after the first copulation.

The female lays the egg with the pointed end first. She takes it up immediately on her feet and covers it with her abdominal flap. The male responds with "dabbling," reaches with his bill under the abdominal flap of the female, and both birds utter "long calls" and attack their neighbors more frequently. From the time of arrival in the rookery until egg-laying the males have spent an average 19 days on land and the females 14 days. The female incubates the egg for several hours after egg-laying. During this period both mates "dabble" often and utter "long-calls" as soon as the egg is visible. After 2–3 hours the female lets the egg roll from her feet and the male pushes it with his bill onto his feet and starts incubating. The female goes to sea the following day and will return 12–21 days later. The male in the meantime stays in his territory, which occupies only 1 m². After her return, the female spends 1–2 days at the beach before she relieves the male. She utters "long calls" as soon as she has reached the vicinity of her mate, and he answers. The female approaches her partner and will call again if she does not find him right away. The male answers, and both greet each other with calls, "dabbling" and "high-pointing," and together they attack neighbors. The male transfers the egg to the female and leaves after 2–3 hours. He has lost about 5 kg weight since his arrival 4–6 weeks before. In the morning after the relief the male leaves the rookery. He will return 2–3 weeks later to relieve the female.

The egg is incubated for 54–56 days. The female covers 24 days, broken up into three periods, including the initial incubation and the time immediately preceding hatching. The males incubate for 31 days, divided into two shifts of 19 and 12 days. This amounts to 57% of the incubation time. If one partner does not return, the other incubates for as long as 35 days.

When hatching is imminent, and the chick peeps in the egg, the

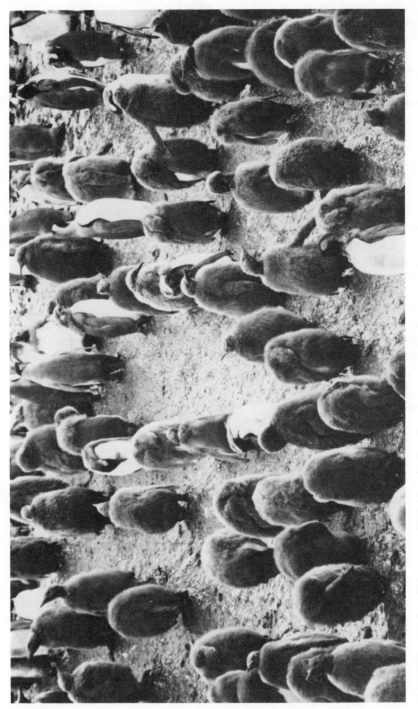

Figure 62   Crèche of king penguins in South Georgia.

parents start to regurgitate food. After hatching the brooding bouts become shorter until the partners relieve each other every three to four days. At the age of 10 days the chicks start to move away from the parents. The chicks form crèches (Fig. 62) at the age of 40 days. In mid-February these can coalesce to form enormous aggregations. The chicks are fed by their parents for 10 months. They grow fast initially and reach adult size at the end of the summer. Their weight is then 12 kg. During the winter they no longer grow, but lose one-third of their body weight. The following spring the chicks receive more food once again. They gain weight again, molt, and start to fledge in late November (South Georgia) or October (Iles Crozet; Despin et al. 1972).

The main predator of the king penguin is the leopard seal. It frequents the coasts of South Georgia in winter and hunts king and gentoo penguins at their landing beaches with great success. Almost 24% of the breeding king penguins and close to 17% of the non-breeders were lost during one year. The mortality of chicks was particularly high in winter (May through October). Chicks that are weakened by hunger become victims of giant petrels (*Macronectes giganteus*). Of 2500 eggs laid, 2100 chicks survived the first year. This is 16% mortality. The other birds in the king penguin rookery are primarily scavengers. They include brown skuas (*Catharacta lonnbergi*), Dominican gulls (*Larus dominicanus*) and sheathbills (*Chionis alba*). On Heard Island, where breeding king penguins increased from 21 in 1963 to 124 in 1971, presumably due to immigration, chick mortality is very high (Budd 1975).

King penguins typically dive to depths of 50 m, and sometimes to more than 240 m (Kooyman et al. 1982).

# Chapter 6

# THE CRESTED PENGUINS _____

Six species of penguins carry yellow plumes on their heads. They comprise the genus *Eudyptes*. The taxonomy of the crested penguins is still unsettled. All species breed on the surface, although some may prefer cover, notably the Fjordland crested penguin. Thus they are set apart from the burrowing species of the genus *Spheniscus* (see next chapter). Four species are confined to the New Zealand seas. These are the Fjordland crested penguin, Snares Island crested penguin, royal penguin, and erect-crested penguin. Of these, two occur only on one island each: the Snares Island penguin on the island of the same name, and the royal penguin on Macquarie Island. The remaining two species, rockhopper and macaroni penguins, breed in more southern latitudes.

## ROCKHOPPER PENGUIN

The rockhopper penguin, *Eudyptes chrysocome* ( = *crestatus*, Fig. 63), derives its name from its gait. Its breeding biology on Macquarie Island (54° 30′S, 159° E) has been described by Warham (1963 and 1972a). "Several hundred thousand" rockhopper penguins are nesting there in addition to the 2.5 million royal penguins and about 50,000 king penguins. The rockhoppers stay at Macquarie from spring to fall, and spend 6 months at sea. Males have a larger bill, and are also heavier (2.7 kg on average) than females (2.5 kg).

Figure 63    Rockhopper penguin, Falkland Islands.

Three different classes of adult birds and immature penguins of three different ages are ashore during the breeding season. It lasts from mid-October to early March (on the Falkland Islands, the rockhoppers arrive in September). The adult penguins comprise breeders, unsuccessful breeders, and non-breeders. Among the immature birds there are two-to-three year olds who are not yet sexually mature, yearlings with their juvenile plumage, and chicks of the year. Rockhoppers breed at 3 years of age, and live for 25–30 years.

The males arrive first in the rookery and occupy a nest site; the females come ashore on the same day or up to 14 days later. Usually the mates of the previous year form a pair again. Copulations are most frequent between November 2 and 5. The eggs are laid between November 7 and 18 and are incubated by both parents for a long spell each. After 32 to 34 days of incubation the chicks hatch between December 17 and 25. After three weeks the guard stage ends, and the chicks gather in crèches. From February 24 through March 10 the chicks leave the rookery. They are then 70 days old. The successful breeders leave the rookery at the same time and fatten up at sea in preparation for the molt. In late March they arrive again at their nests, where they molt during the month of April. By late April they leave the rookery again and spend the winter at sea. (Rockhoppers breeding on the Falkland Islands have been seen up to 100 miles from land during their 5 months at sea.) One male was found at Palmer Station, about 1100 km south of the nearest breeding colonies near Cape Horn (Matthew 1982).

The unsuccessful breeders who have lost their eggs at some time between egg-laying and hatching will leave the rookery and then appear again. They may move about as pairs, or pair with a new partner. But no news eggs are laid.

Among the successful breeders the females incubate the egg after laying, and the males leave the rookery. The males have then spent an average of 33 days in the rookery, and will stay at sea for 12 days.

The males return and relieve the females at the nest who have incubated for 14–15 days on the average and have been in the rookery for 33–45 days without feeding. The males now incubate for 9–16 days until they are relieved by the females about two days before the chicks hatch.

The clutch consists of a small first egg and a larger second one. The first egg is 30–50% smaller than the bigger one and is often lost before hatching time. If a chick hatches from the small one, it will die at the age of 2–5 days, and only the larger chick will be reared. After the chicks have hatched, the male stays for an average of 26 days at the nest while the female obtains food regularly.

At the age of 3 weeks the chicks form crèches. They then weigh 900 grams on the average. One to three days after the chicks have moved from the nest to the crèche, the parent birds start to spend all day in the ocean. They feed their chicks from late afternoon into the night. Pettingill (1960) described the behavior of the crèched chicks in a rookery on the Falkland Islands. He had earlier observed that only 1 chick is reared and that the parents recognize their chicks individually in the crèches. The chicks reach the adult weight of more than 2.5 kg after less than two months. By mid-February they have molted completely and leave the rookery at the age of 70 days.

Rockhopper penguins have a rich repertoire of courtship behavior patterns and communication at the nest. This includes mutual preening, depositing of pebbles at the nest by the male, lateral head quivering with grass (as nesting material) in the bill, bowing, hunched posture, mutual "trumpeting" with stretched-out head and open bill, and the "male court-ship display," corresponding to the "ecstatic" display of other penguins. This display becomes the "mutual courtship display" if the female participates.

In its northernmost rookeries, the rockhopper penguin breeds 3.5 months earlier than at the southern end of its range. The peak of egg laying (50% of pairs have laid 1 egg, and 50% have 2) occurs in September on Tristan da Cunha and Amsterdam Islands (about 38° S), but in De-cember on Heard and Kerguelen Islands (about 50° and 54° S). The peak of egg-laying at these different rookeries is correlated with the average annual sea temperature: at Tristan da Cunha and Amsterdam Island this temperature is about +15° C; at Kerguelen +2° C and at Heard Islands about +1° C. The sea temperature near the intermediate rookeries at Campbell, Antipodes, and Macquarie Islands is +6°–+8° C, and the egg laying peak occurs in the first half of November, between the two men-tioned extremes of September and December. As a general rule, for each rise of mean sea temperature by two centigrades the peak of egg laying advances about 10 days (Warham 1972).

## MACARONI PENGUIN

The macaroni penguin (*Eudyptes chrysolophus*) and royal penguin (*E. schle-geli*) are closely related; indeed they are now considered merely morphs of the same species (Jouventin 1982). Both have long drooping golden tufts on their head, but they differ in their throat which is black in the macaroni (Fig. 64), and white in the royal penguin (Fig. 65).

Vast colonies of macaroni penguins, estimated at 40 million birds are on South Georgia and the outlying islands, such as Bird, Willis, and Trinity Islands. Some breed among chinstrap penguins on Elephant and Clarence Islands. In the macaroni penguin the female incubates the eggs first, as do rockhopper and royal penguins. The displays of the macaroni penguin have been described by Matthews (1929) and Dowres et al. (1959).

## ROYAL PENGUIN

There are two and a half million royal penguins (Fig. 66), and all breed on Macquarie Island. They have filled all available space between the tus-sock grass from the beach to elevations reaching up to 200 m, and for a distance of 1 km inland. Warham (1971) has studied the breeding behavior of the royal penguins.

The males weigh about 4.5 kg and the females 4.0 kg. The bill of the male is longer and thicker than that of the female, and the face is white

Figure 64  Macaroni penguin, Nelson Island, South Shetland Islands.

in the male and gray in the female. The males return from the sea in mid-September, followed by the females. After the eggs are laid between October 10 and 30 the male stays for several days. Following that, the female incubates for 14 days, until she is relieved by the male, who incubates for 2 more weeks. The chicks hatch between November 21 and December 10, when both parents are present. The male guards the single chick (the other egg does not hatch) for 10–20 days, while the female feeds it during that time. Then the chick joins a crèche, and the male leaves for the sea. The chick is now fed by both parents. The chicks leave the colony for the sea in late January. The adults follow them for their pre-molt fattening up. They stay at sea for 5 weeks and spend 1 more month molting and fasting. After completing the molt in late March, they leave again. After May 15 no royal penguins are present on or near Macquarie Island.

The displays of the royal penguin are very similar to those of the closely related macaroni penguin. They include mutual preening, quivering (head shaking while bent down to the nest), bowing (with throbbing calls), the "shoulders-hunched attitude" before nest-relief, trumpeting (mutual loud braying when meeting at the nest), and the head-swing (the head with open bill is waved back and forth, with vocalizations; this display often follows disturbances, and is similar to the loud mutual display of Adélie penguin).

Figure 65    Royal penguin.

Figure 66    Rookery of the royal penguin on Macquarie Island.

Mortality among the chicks is high: in a colony of 2000 pairs only 760 chicks fledged per year (Carrick and Ingham 1967). Eggs are taken by brown skuas (*Catharacta lonnbergi*), and wekas (*Gallirallus australis*). Giant petrels (*Macronectes giganteus*) take peripheral chicks and fledglings during their departure. Southern elephant seals may crawl into a colony and squash eggs, chicks and adults. New Zealand fur seals (*Arctocephalus forsteri*) hunt royal penguins, but pinnipeds, including Hooker's sea lion (*Neophoca hookeri*) and leopard seals (*Hydrurga leptonyx*), are negligible as predators of this penguin species. In the past, the royal penguins have also been exploited by man. At the beginning of the 20th century a Mr. Hatch, operating under a license granted by Tasmania, harvested 100,000 royal penguins annually. Oil-rich yearlings and adults returning to molt were used. Ten men, using several digesters, could process over 2000 penguins per day, yielding about 2500 liters of oil. The digesters can still be seen among the royal penguins at the Nuggets (Fig. 2) and in the king penguin rookery at Lusitania Bay.

## FJORDLAND CRESTED PENGUIN

The Fjordland crested penguin, *Eudyptes pachyrhynchus* (Fig. 67), and the Snares Island penguin, *E. robustus*, (Fig. 68) are very similar, and in the past *E. robustus* was considered merely a subspecies of *E. pachyrhynchus* (Falla, 1935). But the two penguins are morphologically distinct, no hybrids have been reported, and their reproductive isolation is temporal: the Fjordland penguin lays her eggs in July, the Snares Island penguin in September and October. The Snares Island penguin has a pronounced fleshy fillet of pink or white skin at the base of the bill. In the Fjordland penguin the cheek feathers have gray bases, leading to the appearance of gray mottling when a bird is displaying or ruffling its feathers.

The Fjordland crested penguin breeds on the southwest coast of the South Island of New Zealand, and on Stewart and Solander Island (46° 55'S, 166° 50'E) both south of New Zealand. Its nests are found under thick cover, notably New Zealand flax (*Phormium cookianum*) and Kie-Kie (*Freycinetia banksii*). The birds are very shy and hard to see in the dense vegetation. Warham (1974a) studied this species for 6 seasons.

The birds are ashore breeding for about 20 weeks from early July to late November. Their continuous time at sea can be estimated from the growth of barnacles on their tails: *Lepas* barnacles are about 1 cm long, when the penguins arrive. It takes 3–4 weeks to grow to that size. Hence the Fjordland penguin does not spend as much time at sea as has been previously assumed. Warham (1974) observed the first bird ashore on June 12. As in other species, males arrive before females. At the end of July all nest sites are occupied. Egg-laying peaks around August 6. From arrival to egg-laying the birds fast; the males' weight drops from 4.5 to 3.5 kg, and that of the females from 4 to about 3 kg.

Figure 67    Fjordland crested penguin (Photo: Jules Tapper, Invercargill, New Zealand).

The nest is a shallow cup with some leaves and sticks as lining. It is located in a hollow at the base of, or under, roots, rocks, or boulders in the forest. The males advertise their territory with vertical head-waving, and vertical trumpeting.

Copulations start in early August. The same partners form pairs in subsequent years, and use the same nest, although the nest site is changed more often than the partner.

The first eggs were found about July 26 and all eggs are laid by August 14. Eighty to 90% of the nests have 2 eggs, the rest only 1. The second egg is larger, and is laid 3–6 days after the first. During egg-laying

Figure 68    Snares Island penguin (Photo: Frank S. Todd).

both parents are present. Incubation starts after the second egg has been laid. After the clutch is complete, the female leaves and the male incubates for 13 days. Then the female takes over for about 13 days. The number of females on eggs peaks about August 23. By then the males have fasted 40–45 days, having lost 27% of their body weight. The eggs lose 0.36 gram per day during incubation. Lost eggs are not rolled back into the nest.

The eggs hatch after about 33.5 (31–36) days of incubation. There is no set sequence in the hatching of the 2 eggs. First and second eggs are equally often infertile. The hatching peak occurs around September 9, with most chicks hatching between September 4 and 14. Infertile eggs may be incubated for more than 3 weeks after their predicted hatching date. Either of the 2 eggs is lost equally often. As a rule, crested penguins do not re-lay after loss of their clutch. During hatching lone males or both parents are present, and only rarely lone females. Of the pairs that lay eggs, 79% hatch, on the average, at least 1 chick.

The 3 weeks after hatching comprise the guard stage. The males fast and stay at the nest during the day. At night they are joined by the females who feed the chicks. Newly-hatched chicks hide under the parent's brood pouch, sitting on its feet.

On the average, 67% of the pairs that lay eggs are successful in rearing chicks to within 1 week of the termination of the guard stage (range: 42-87% in 4 different years).

At 3 weeks of age (about September 30) the chicks form small crèches and the guarding male leaves for the sea to forage. The female feeds the young, usually in the evening. The parent bird, returning with food, stops at the nest, calls, and bows, and follows this with forward and vertical trumpeting. The chick approaches the parent from a crèche or from cover, cheeps and waves its flippers, and then begs for food. The adult bird regurgitates food some 6–8 times in a feeding sequence. Around October 14, the crèches disperse, but re-form when danger, in the shape of people, introduced mustelids, or fur seals (*Arctocephalus forsteri*), threatens. In November, when the male has replenished his own food reserves at sea, he participates more in the feeding of the chick.

The average time required for fledging is 75 days, and 50–64% of eggs laid resulted in chicks alive at fledging time. Of chicks hatched, 81% were observed to survive at least to a period just before fledging. All pairs had only 1 chick during the post-guard stage, although 31–52 percent of the pairs hatched both eggs. The chicks are fed primarily cephalopods, and some euphausiids. The first chicks leave for the sea in mid-November. The exodus peaks around November 23, with little variation from year to year.

After their chicks have left, the breeders spend 60–80 days at sea. From December 15 to January 9 no Fjordland penguins are present on the breeding areas. Fattened-up birds appear ashore for the molt in early February. The males weigh 4936 grams on the average, and the females 4820 grams. The molt is completed after 25 days. The weight of the males has then dropped to 3000 grams, and that of the females to 2520 grams.

Mortality of chicks is mainly due to chilling in heavy rains and storms. Some chicks are drowned by water flooding the nest. There are no natural predators on land. Introduced stoats (*Mustela erminea*) pierce eggs and dismember chicks.

The displays are similar to those of the other crested penguins, and Warham (1974) stresses the impressive individual variation of sounds and movements, which may be a very important factor in recognition (see also Jouventin 1982).

The main displays are vertical and forward trumpeting, vertical head swinging, bowing, and "shoulders-hunched attitude." In general, the vocalizations are loud, presumably an adaptation to the forest habitat, where a pair usually is in visual contact with only one other pair. Fjordland penguins have an alarm call that is a high-pitched squeal of about one second duration and resembles that of the rockhopper penguin. This squeal is uttered when a person approaches, or when 2 penguins are fighting.

## SNARES ISLAND PENGUIN

The Snares Island penguin (Fig. 68) has been studied by Warham (1974b) on the Snares Islands (48 S, 165 E) for six seasons. The males are larger and heavier than the females, and this size difference is already noticeable in yearlings and, perhaps, in chicks. On the Snares Islands there are 135 breeding colonies, with an average of 44 fledglings produced in each. The total number of birds of this species is estimated at 30,000 to 50,000. Snares crested penguins start to breed at the age of 6 years.

The breeding cycle starts with the return of the males in the first 3 weeks of September. The females arrive 7–8 days later. The colonies have a density of 2 nests per m². The first egg is small, and 4.5 days later a larger egg is laid. After laying, both parents stay at the nest for 10 days, and take turns in incubating, until the male leaves for the ocean. Then the female incubates for 12 days, followed by the male for 11 days. The male is present when the chicks hatch. He defends them for 3 weeks, while the female feeds the chicks every day. Only 1 chick survives the guard stage. After 3 weeks this surviving chick joins a crèche. Both parents feed the chick while in the crèche. It remains close to the nest site. At the age of 75 days the chicks leave for the sea. The adults leave at the same time.

The breeding birds stay at sea and fatten up for the molt for 70 days and the colonies are deserted from mid-February through late March. This is much longer than in the more southern species of crested penguins, the rockhopper and macaroni penguins. The molt is complete in late April; by April 26 the number of birds returning to sea is reaching a peak.

Inclement weather, primarily rainstorms, cause most chick mortality, while predation and parasites are insignificant. The courtship displays are essentially the same as in the rockhopper and royal penguins. Measurements of Snares Island penguins are given in Stonehouse (1971).

## ERECT-CRESTED PENGUIN

The third crested penguin belonging to this group is the erect-crested penguin, *Eudyptes sclateri* (Fig. 69). All 3 birds were once thought to belong to 1 species (Falla, 1935). The erect-crested penguin has a fleshy edge

Figure 69    Erect-crested penguin (Photo: John Warham).

around the base of the bill and is slightly larger than the other two species. The underside of the flipper has much bluish-black on its leading edge and tip. This species breeds on the Antipodes and Bounty Islands, and in small numbers on Campbell Island.

Richdale (1941, 1950) described the breeding biology of the erect-crested penguin on the mainland of the South Island of New Zealand, essentially an atypical situation. For eight years a female arrived at the nesting site around September 25. Three weeks later she laid a small and a large egg, always at exactly the same spot. The courtship displays are basically the "ecstatic" display with open bill, and one that resembles the "quiet mutual" display of the Adélie penguin.

Warham (1972b) studied the erect-crested penguin at Antipodes Island (49° 40′S, 178° 50′E). The first information about the breeding cycle at this site came from survivors of 2 shipwrecks. In 1893, 11 survivors of the iron barge *Spirit of the Dawn* lived here for 87 days, mostly on penguins, before being rescued. They saw the first penguin on September 5 and large numbers thereafter. The first egg was found on October 2, and many more on October 3. The sailors also noted that the second egg within the body of slaughtered penguins was larger than the first one. A smaller species of penguin—the rockhopper—was reported to have arrived a month later. On March 13, 1908, the ship *President Felix Faure* went aground and the sailors reported that the penguins disappeared about Good Friday (April 17).

Today we know that the males arrive during the second week of September, the females in mid-September. The nests are on flat ground and 66 cm apart, on the average (range: 46–91 cm). Egg-laying peaks on October 12, and hatching about November 17 after about 35 days incubation. The chicks enter crèches around December 10, and adults and chicks depart about January 30. The last birds leave around April 20.

The molt starts during the third week of February. Fifty percent of the birds are molting by March 11. After 4 weeks the molting is completed, and the birds leave for the sea, where they spend the winter.

The males are about 17% heavier than the females. Their bills are 11–16% longer, deeper and wider. Warham described 20 display patterns. They are similar to those of the rockhopper and royal penguins, and include mutual preening, quivering, bowing, shoulders-hunched posture, trumpeting, head-swinging, and mutual display (the female responds to the male's head-swinging by stretching up to his bill, and growling).

# Chapter 7

# THE BANDED PENGUINS _____

The banded penguins of the genus *Spheniscus* are familiar to the public, since the black-footed (or jackass) penguin (*S. demersus*) from South Africa and the Humboldt penguin (*S. humboldti*) from the coasts of Peru and Chile have been displayed in zoos for a long time.

The genus *Spheniscus* comprises 4 species. In addition to the black-footed and Humboldt penguins there are the Magellanic (*S. magellanicus*) and Galapagos penguins (*S. mendiculus*). The banded penguins tend to breed either in burrows, which they dig out themselves, or simply under or between overhanging rocks, roots and the like. The Humboldt and black-footed penguins are the producers of the commercially important guano.

## BLACK-FOOTED PENGUIN

The composition of the diet of the *black-footed penguin* (Fig. 70) has been investigated by Rand (1960). The reason for his study was to determine whether this penguin species competes seriously for commercially important small fish. The stomach contents of 247 black-footed penguins consisted of 25 species of fish, 3 species of squid, 18 crustacean species and 1 polychaete. The birds had an average of 115 grams of food in their stomach, their own body weight being slightly under 3 kg. The number

Figure 70    Black-footed penguin on its two-egg clutch.

of penguins on 8 islands was estimated at 103,000 (123,000 in 1975 by Siegfried et al.), consuming about 7000 tons of food each year. Of this, only 42%, or 2900 tons, are fish. Therefore, the black-footed penguin is not considered to be detrimental to the fisheries, especially since it is economically beneficial as a producer of guano.

Today, 70,000 black-footed penguins are left on Dassen Island, and the total population is estimated at 176,000, against a former 5 million. The straw-necked ibis is a predator of this species' eggs. Eggleton and Siegfried (1979) studied the displays of the jackass penguin. To avoid heat stress, it comes ashore during the cool and dark hours, and communicates with loud calls. High insolation has favored burrow-nesting (Fig. 71), which in turn has led to an absence of chick crèches. Burrow sites may be a limiting resource. Nest building appears to be a remnant of surface breeding.

Being situated near a major shipping lane, the black-footed penguins of South Africa are in constant danger of oil spills such as that in 1983 from the tanker *Castillo de Bellver* that broke up west of Saldanha Bay, the site of a penguin colony on Marcus Island. Groups of 50 or more jackass penguins have been observed as far as 50 km from the islands they use for breeding (Siegfried et al. 1975).

The three South American species of banded penguins have been

Figure 71   Nest burrows of the black-footed penguin. Marcus Island, South Africa.

Figure 72    Magellanic penguin.

Figure 73   Magellanic penguin at burrow in dense tussock grass. Cape Horn, Chile, January 1983.

Figure 74    Magellanic penguins at their nest burrows. Punta Tombo, Argentina.

Figure 75    Magellanic penguin with its two-egg clutch.

little studied. The Humboldt penguin, in particular, (Fig. 76) is so little known that its rookeries have only very recently been surveyed (Modinger 1983).

## MAGELLANIC PENGUIN

Magellanic penguins (Fig. 72) breed in burrows in the ground (Fig. 73) and under bushes (Fig. 74). They lay their eggs in early October (Fig. 75), and the peak of hatching occurs around November 15; there is also a fall peak of breeding. Actually, the birds stay in the area for most of the year. Incubation lasts 39 days (Boswall and Prytherch 1972). At Punta Tombo in Argentina (44° 00′S, 62° 20′W) there are over a million birds in one rookery which covers 2.23 square kilometers (Fig. 76). The number of nests per 100 m² varies from 1 or 2 to 80, with an average of 20 nests per 100 m². Boswall and Prytherch (1972) estimated a total rookery size of 446,000 breeding pairs. Others estimated 600,000 pairs (King and Olrog, in Boswall and Pyrtherch 1972) or "over 200,000" (Conway 1971). Other rookeries of Magellanic penguins are located further south on the islands of Tora and Torita (45° 05′S, 66° 01′W), and on Isla de los Estados (54° 43′S, 64° 02′W). Except for a small colony of 50 pairs south of Punta Ninfas (43° 05′S, 64° 30′W), the frequently visited rookery at Punta Tombo appears to be the northernmost. In the Straits of Magellan and on the Falkland Islands are more breeding colonies. A list of all known rookeries of the Magellanic penguin is available at the Alexander Library of the Edward Grey Institute in Oxford, England.

Magellanic penguins are shy near Punta Arenas in Southern Chile, but they do not flee from people at Punta Tombo. They use their burrows—which can be 1–2 m deep—for protection from predators and heat. The Patagonian fox preys on these penguins.

The chicks do not grow as fast as those of other species, since there are few climatic or predation pressures. They fledge at the age of 3 months; the fledglings are dull in color, have no bands, but a white eye-stripe.

In 1982 the Magellanic penguin became the target of potential commercial exploitation: the Hinode Penguin S. A. proposed to kill 48,000 penguins annually for two years. The skins were to be used for gloves and other luxury leather products, and the meat as human food.

## HUMBOLDT (PERUVIAN) PENGUIN

The Humboldt penguin, *Spheniscus humboldti* (Fig. 77), formerly common in zoos, is one of the more heat-adapted penguins, as bare, fleshy areas below and behind the eye attest. Fledglings that have no black stripes on the chest already have the bare skin on the head. Humboldt penguins occur on the coasts of Peru and Chile from 6° 30′S to 34° 00′S (Modinger

Figure 76   Rookery of Magellanic penguins. Punta Tombo, Argentina.

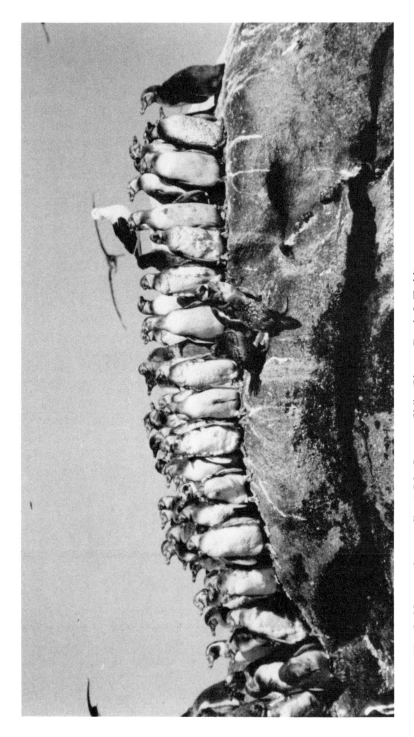

Figure 77   Humboldt penguins (yearlings) Isla Concon, Chile (Photo: Frank S. Todd).

Figure 78    Galapagos penguin (Photo: Claus Koenig).

1983), but its rookeries and total population are only scantily known, though a census of the species is currently being taken in Peru and Chile. The total population at present is estimated under 20,000 birds (Modinger 1983). Formerly there were "hundreds of thousands" on the bird islands off Peru (Johnson 1965), with guano up to 100 m thick. Providing extremely rich fertilizer, these guano penguins, along with Peruvian boobies, Peruvian gannets, and guano cormorants were known as the "billion-dollar-birds." Recently, their food base has been destroyed by over-fishing the anchovettas. This is in addition to the natural disasters that occur every 7–8 years when the cold, northward-flowing Peru current veers away from the coast. It is then displaced by the warmer Pacific Equatorial Counter-Current moving south off Colombia. Upwelling ceases, and during such an "El Niño year" millions of birds die due to ensuing shortage of fish.

## GALAPAGOS PENGUIN

The Galapagos penguin, *Spheniscus mendiculus* (Fig. 78), is the most tropical of all penguins. It lives at the equator and betrays several features of adaptation to a warm climate: small size (Bergmann's rule!) long flippers and bill, (Allen's rule!) and large naked areas on the face for heat exchange. It only sometimes digs burrows like the other species of the genus *Spheniscus*; instead it uses cracks in lava for nesting sites. This species breeds only on 2 large islands, Isabela and Fernandina, of the Galapagos group, where the water is coldest and most productive. Boersma, who studied the Galapagos penguin intensively (1975, 1976), estimates the total population at about 15,000 birds. Males, on average, weigh 2119 grams and females 1878 grams.

Boersma (1976) described the adaptations of the Galapagos penguin to a daily routine that includes as extremes feeding in waters that are cooled by the Cromwell Current and displaying on land at +40° C. Although local water temperatures measured by Boersma ranged from +15 to +28° C, the water around the Galapagos Islands, especially to the west, is cooler than elsewhere near the equator. From October to December the temperature at a depth of 10 meters averages +20° C around these islands, while it reaches +25 or even +30° C in other parts of the Pacific Ocean (Barkley 1968). Surface water temperatures on the west side of the Galapagos archipelago can be as "low" as +17° C in Nov./Dec. (Stevenson et al. 1970).

The penguins spend the day foraging at sea and sleep on land during the night. In the water, the body temperature is 2° C lower than on land, but heat loss in water can be counteracted by swimming on the surface, so that the dark plumage on the back absorbs solar radiation. On land, Galapagos penguins keep the lightly feathered parts of the flippers and feet shaded by the heavily insulated back and body, so that feet and flipper undersides can act as cooling surfaces. Standing birds keep their flippers lifted at 45° from the body. When prone, the flippers droop at the bird's sides. In addition to this postural thermoregulation, the blood-flow to the undersides of feet and flippers also helps to regulate heat losses and gains. Boersma describes a pair that deserted their clutch in intense solar radiation, panted heavily and retreated to the ocean. When the birds returned in the afternoon, their eggs were cooked. Molting birds, in particular, avoid overheating by seeking shade, and keep out of the water to avoid rapid cooling. The Galapagos penguin molts twice a year, which is unique among penguins. This is presumably so as to keep the plumage in good shape for the extraordinary twin task of providing insulation against heat on land and cold in the water.

The courtship displays of the Galapagos penguin include mutual preening, flipper patting, in which the bills of the two sexes touch, as a prelude to copulation, and bill dueling.

The occurrence and timing of breeding is "erratic and unpredictable" (Boersma 1976). The Galapagos penguin breeds throughout the year, though most eggs are laid in August and September. A normal clutch has 2 eggs. Lost eggs are hardly ever replaced. The birds start incubating after laying the first egg. Males take incubation turns averaging 1.9 days, while females average 2.0 days. The eggs are incubated for 38–42 days. The chicks are brooded for 2 weeks, during which they appear to be unable to thermoregulate themselves. The chick stage lasts just under 60 days. One-fourth of the population breeds twice a year.

Breeding success ranges from 0–54%, averaging 20% over 3 years. This high rate of mortality can be due to tidal flooding, breakage of eggs, or predation.

The predators of eggs and chicks are the Sally Lightfoot crab (*Grapsus grapsus*), the rice rat (*Oryzomys nesoryzomis narboroughi*), and Galapagos snakes (*Dromicus slevini* and *D. dorsalis*). Predators of adults are the Galapagos hawk (*Buteo galapagoensis*), short-eared owl (*Asio flammeus*), barn owl (*Tyto alba*) and feral house cats and dogs.

Before mating the Galapagos penguin needs to gain about 26% of its body weight. Before and after molting are the times when food may be a limiting factor for this species. The food resources from the productive Cromwell Current are unpredictable and in consequence molting is the time of highest mortality.

The Galapagos penguin has adapted to its unpredictable environment in several ways. First, it is a food generalist to the extent that it takes many species of fish at different depths and locations, as long as they are under about 15 mm long. Second, it does not have a fixed annual breeding cycle, and third, it lays 2 or 3 clutches, totaling an average of 4–6 eggs, per year.

# Chapter 8

## FAIRY PENGUINS

The fairy or little blue penguin, *Eudyptula minor* (Fig. 79), is the smallest penguin species and occurs on New Zealand and on the South Coast of Australia. Many authors consider the white-flippered penguin (Fig. 80) of the Banks Peninsula of New Zealand's South Island a separate species, *E. albosignata*. Both species breed in burrows and have essentially the same breeding cycle.

The breeding biology of the fairy penguin is well known, thanks to the studies of O'Brien, Richdale, Warham, and Kinsky.

The bird spends the winter near its breeding colony, or even in the colony itself—though the nests are spaced so widely along the beach and the slopes above, that the term "colony" applies only in the loosest sense.

Most of the eggs are laid from mid-August to mid-September, but clutches can be found from July to December. The nest is located under outcropping rocks, or in burrows that can be up to 1 m deep. It is lined with twigs, grass, or fern. The clutch consists of two eggs which are incubated for 39 days. Both parents take turns at incubating, with the female taking a slightly greater share.

The chicks hatch in October and November and weigh 40 grams at hatching. After 1 week their weight has increased five-fold, and at the age of 2 weeks they weigh 400 grams. From their second day they are fed only in the evening. At each feeding a chick receives 25–150 grams of food.

Figure 79   Little blue penguin, Somes Island, New Zealand (Photo: New Zealand Wildlife Service).

Figure 80   White-flippered penguin (Photo: New Zealand Wildlife Service).

There is considerable difference between siblings: one often receives 4–8 times as much food as the other.

The male fairy penguin has a larger bill. During the nest relief both mates call with their heads raised, but without lateral head-waving. Warham (1958) distinguishes a "half-trumpet" and a "full-trumpet". The nest relief takes place in the evening. Immediately afterwards the chicks are fed. The parent bird leaves the nest in the early morning hours.

The chicks pass through 3 stages: During the first, they are guarded day and night. This lasts 10–22 days. The second stage starts during the third week of age. Only one of the parents is present, and that only during the night. During the day the chick is left by itself. Finally, at four weeks of age, the chick is left unattended day and night. The chicks leave the colony and head for the ocean when they are 49–60 days old.

Figure 81    Habitat of little blue penguin: Somes Island in Wellington Harbor, New Zealand.

The chicks hatch with down feathers, which they exchange for the second down plumage at the age of 7 days. At 28 days, they start to molt into the final plumage. At the same time the chick reaches almost the maximal weight before leaving the colony: 960 grams, or 24 times its hatching weight.

On Somes Island (Fig. 81) in Wellington Harbour, where Kinsky worked with fairy penguins, there are no predators, and they still lost 42% and 53% of their clutches in two subsequent years. Of these, 90% were lost during the egg stage. In contrast to Somes Island, Warham's fairy penguins in Australia were preyed upon by fur seals, harriers, gulls, snakes and lizards. The little blue penguin is the only penguin species that counts the automobile among its "predators": road kills are frequent in Australia.

Before molting, fairy penguins fatten up. There are molting birds from December through March, with a peak of molting between mid-January and mid-February. The penguins are on land day and night and stay during the night in their own burrows or other shelters. Their body weight may decrease from 1500 grams to 850 grams during the 15 days of molting. During the molt ectoparasites become very visible. Richdale counted 187 ticks (*Ixodes eudyptidis*) on one animal.

After the molting period the little blue penguins go to sea, and in late March they start to return. Many arrive as pairs. These are pairs that have bred together during the previous year, and they stay near their former nest.

The fairy penguin of Australia has a slightly different breeding cycle. It has been studied on Phillip Island near Melbourne (Reilly and Cullen 1979, 1981).

There the penguins are present in the colony throughout the year. After their molt (February to April), the birds spend much time at sea, but they come ashore from time to time. Breeding starts typically in August or September, but sometimes as early as June or even May. Seven weeks before egg-laying 50% of the males are ashore. The number of birds ashore peaks 7 and 4 weeks and 1 week before egg-laying, suggesting some energetic periodicity. Like other northern penguin species (see banded penguins), the little blue penguin has an extended breeding season. Reilly and Cullen (1981) found eggs from May through December, although the laying peak was in September and October. The egg-laying period (13–18 weeks) was much longer than in New Zealand (14 weeks, Kinsky 1960) or Tasmania (8–11 weeks, Hodgdon 1975). Virtually all clutches that were lost from May to June were replaced, while no re-laying occurred if November or December clutches were lost.

The incubation period is 35 days. The chick is attended by either of the parents for 15 days and thereafter left unguarded. At 5 weeks of age it starts to wander from its burrow, and after 7.5–10 weeks the chicks leave for the sea.

The breeding success can be divided into hatching success (number of eggs producing chicks), fledging success (number of chicks surviving until fledging), and "egg success" (number of eggs resulting in fledged young). Hatching success in Reilly's and Cullen's study was 64%, fledging success 41%, and egg success 26%. Egg success was best for eggs laid between August and November (27–33%).

The mortality of adult penguins at Phillip Island is 14.2% per year and the life expectancy of a bird breeding for the first time is 6.5 years (Reilly and Cullen 1979).

## WHITE-FLIPPERED PENGUIN

The white-flippered penguin, *Eudyptula albosignata*, was split off from the fairy penguin by O. Finsch in 1874, but today there is a tendency to not recognize it as a separate species. It breeds primarily on the Banks Peninsula of New Zealand's South Island.

The white-flippered penguin has been studied by O'Brien (1940). The male has a heavier beak in this penguin, too. The breeding colony becomes active during the third week of September. Nests are located in burrows and constructed from twigs, Mesembryanthemum, and grass. The first eggs were found on September 17. The clutch consists of 2 eggs, just like in the little blue penguin, and is incubated for 38 days. Both sexes take turns at incubating. The males return from the sea between 19:45 and 20:00 hrs and relieve the females. The females in turn leave soon after that and at 01:00 hrs all are at sea again. Around 03:45 hrs all females have returned and take over the clutch. Thus, the females incubate for 21 hours in every 24-hour period. As in the little blue penguin the breeding season lasts from mid-September through late January. In O'Brien's study 57% of the eggs were deserted, and 80% of the chicks died. The adults started to molt on January 9.

# Chapter 9

# THE YELLOW-EYED PENGUIN_

The yellow-eyed penguin, *Megadyptes antipodes*, (Fig. 82) inhabits Southern New Zealand coasts and islands to the south, ranging to the Auckland Islands and Campbell Island. This species does not migrate. It has been considered the most generalized penguin species (Murphy 1959).

Richdale's (1957) work on the population dynamics of the yellow-eyed penguin is a classic. He studied the small breeding colony at the Otago Peninsula on the South Island of New Zealand. There the penguins breed under brush on a steep sand slope. Richdale observed his birds for 18 years. A summary of his findings can be found in Lack (1966).

In 1938/39 the colony consisted of 26 nests. It grew to 82 nests in 1952/53. Richdale considered this higher number as normal for the population, since the penguins had been decimated by human activity prior to his study. In addition to the breeders there were 38% non-breeders on the average. The non-breeders were 1–4 years old.

Forty-eight percent of the females bred at the age of 2 years. Of these, 38% laid only 1 egg. All females bred when 3 years old, and 94% then had 2 eggs. The males started to breed at a later age: only 8% when 2 years old, 35% at 3 years, 68% at 4 years of age, and probably 100% from 5 years on.

Richdale demonstrated that the same breeding pairs raised young together in consecutive years. As a rule, they also used the same nest site

Figure 82   Yellow-eyed penguin. Enderby Island, Auckland Islands.

again and again. Only in 14% of the cases where both mates returned to the colony did they not breed together. Only just under half of the penguins that bred for the first time were born in the colony. The remainder immigrated from other places. On the other hand, Richdale found penguins breeding in other colonies several kilometers away that had been raised in his study colony.

The egg-laying period lasted 3–4 weeks. A particular female would always lay either early or late. The survival rates of early and late chicks were the same, in contrast to passerine birds of the temperate zone. Seventy-eight percent of the eggs hatched, and 76% of the chicks fledged. Overall, 59% of the eggs resulted in fledged young.

The breeding success increases with the age of the females: 32% of the eggs of the two-year-old females hatched, compared with 70% of those of three-year-old first breeders; 82% of the eggs of three-year-old females breeding for the second time hatched, and 87% of those of four-year-old females. The survival rate of the chicks also increased with the age of the parents.

The annual mortality of adults was 13% in Richdale's study. More females than males were lost. The average life expectancy was calculated as 7 years. The 13% loss was balanced by 13% recruitment of three-year-old new breeders. The annual loss during the second and third years of life was 15–16%.

# Chapter 10

## COMPARATIVE ETHOLOGY AND THE EVOLUTION OF PENGUINS___

The adaptive radiation of penguins is generally assumed to have originated in temperate latitudes (40–50° S) in the New Zealand sector (e.g. Jouventin 1982), where today the largest number of species and subspecies as well as the smallest and least differentiated genus, Eudyptula, can still be found. The spread to north and south was accompanied by adaptive changes. Northern species had to cope with heat, solar radiation, and predators, which favored dispersed breeding and the use use of burrows. Antarctic species, on the other hand, faced low temperatures, a short summer season, and limited breeding space that may be frozen and/or snow-covered; these birds thus lacked opportunities to use or dig burrows, but benefited from the absence of land predators. They responded with increased body size, by pairs breeding in extremely close proximity to each other, and by speeding up the breeding cycle. These trends can even be observed within species: Southern subspecies tend to be larger, with shorter body appendages, as in the gentoo penguin; the time from hatching to fledging is 1 week shorter in the most southerly Adélie chicks at Cape Royds than in Adélies in the South Orkney Islands (Taylor 1962). Differences between the species are even more extreme: Adélie penguins fledge in half the time taken by the yellow-eyed penguin, for instance.

These adaptive changes necessitated concomitant adjustments in agonistic behavior, visual displays and vocal communication, breeding strategies, general social behavior and foraging techniques. Even today, the smallest species, such as little and Galapagos penguins, and also the more primitive yellow-eyed penguins are the least colonial, while the two largest, genus Aptenodytes, are the most social, having, in the case of the emperor penguin, dispensed with territoriality at breeding time and having gained the ability to thermoregulate by social means. The Adélie penguin has retained territoriality, but shows the shortest inter-nest distances among the Antarctic pygoscelids (Müller-Schwarze and Müller-Schwarze 1975). Furthermore, it possesses a rich repertoire of social signals.

## CONSEQUENCES OF COLONIAL BREEDING

Colonial breeding in its simplest form may represent utilization of limited space by an increasing population, without any social factors operating *a priori*.

A breeding aggregation, however, will open up new opportunities for its members, such as social foraging, or joint anti-predator defense. At the same time it imposes new constraints, requiring new forms of social signaling in sexual, agonistic and parental contexts, and favoring, if not necessitating, individual recognition. If individuals can increase their "inclusive fitness" (i.e., survival of themselves and their offspring) not only by direct competition with others, but also indirectly by supporting close relatives, joint nest-defense and the sharing of information about food sources will be favored forms of behavior.

## Individual recognition

Individual recognition of offspring by their parents has been demonstrated for Adélies (Penney 1968), emperor (Jouventin et al. 1979) and king penguins (Derenne et al. 1979), and macaroni and rockhopper penguins (Jouventin 1982). Chicks that have been experimentally prevented from identifying themselves to their approaching parents (by having had their bills taped shut) are not fed, and may be pecked as if they were strangers. In Adélie chicks, an individual's song varies during the first 2–3 weeks, but becomes constant at the age of 3 weeks, when crèches form and the recognition of offspring becomes essential (Jouventin 1982). The variation coefficient for syllable length and other features of the song of mates and chicks is small for individuals, but large for populations in emperor and king penguins, ensuring individual recognition. In the Adélie and macaroni penguins, however, the individual songs vary as much as those in the populations. The latter 2 species have nests as aids for recognizing partners and chicks.

## SEXUAL SELECTION

Even though sexual selection has been analysed mostly in polygamous birds, all the processes involved—such as male-male or female-female competition, and male or female choice of mates—may play a role, to varying degrees, in monogamous species too.

In the particularly well-investigated Adélie penguin there is male-male competition early in the season, when males select, occupy, advertise, and defend breeding territories before the females arrive.

Although females usually join their former mates, a female breeding for the first time may choose the better quality male and territory. The better quality territory would minimize predation (i.e., be located in the center of the colony rather than at its periphery), and would be safe from snow drifts or flooding later on (i.e., be located on a ridge or knoll). The male itself can vary in genetic and parental quality (Searcy and Yasukawa 1983), but how the female gauges these qualities is not known. The male's displays, fighting ability and frequency, size, shape, and location of his nest are the most likely factors. There is evidence that multiple features of members of the opposite sex may be used in mate choice of monogamous species (Burley 1981).

In penguins males are generally larger than females and often have heavier bills. The larger bill of the male may be correlated with the slightly different feeding patterns of the sexes, as has been demonstrated for some passerines, woodpeckers and others (Selander 1972), but it may also be promoted by social factors, such as fighting. Thus, both natural selection and sexual selection can be operating in the size dimorphism of the body or its parts. For penguins, the precise mechanisms of such dimorphisms are not known at present. As in many other birds and mammals, the virtual absence of sexual dimorphism in visual markings is correlated with a strong tendency for monogamy. For instance, in Penney's (1968) study, 50–83% of the breeding pairs reunited in the following season. Males were 93% faithful to their territory, and females were faithful to their mates. Monogamy increases inclusive fitness. Faithful pairs raised 12% more chicks than those that changed partners (Penney 1968). In the Adélie penguin sexual dimorphism of body weight is greatest at the beginning of the breeding season when most fighting takes place. Bill size is most dimorph, that of the flippers less so, and the tarsus shows no difference (Ainley and Emison 1972).

## DISPLAYS

The displays are derived from common patterns of locomotion, preening, nest-building, or attack. Abundance, precision and redundancy of agonistic signals are correlated with synchronization and contraction of the breeding cycle (Jouventin 1982). The most complex and most modified (ritualized) agonistic behavior occurs in the Adélie and emperor penguins, the two species in the most extreme Antarctic and with the densest breeding aggregations, although the former fiercely defends territories while the latter has given up not only territorial defense, but even attachment to a breeding site, that the king penguin still has. The males of species with the most synchronized breeding cycles, such as Adélie and chinstrap, have the most elaborate "ecstatic displays." Mutual displays are present in all species, and the intensity of these displays is correlated with the degree of territoriality and aggressiveness of a given species. For instance, the fiercely territorial Adélie and some crested penguins have the most elaborate mutual displays, while the non-territorial emperor has an "almost motionless display" (Jouventin 1982). Within a genus, agonistic signals can vary considerably, from the frequent direct attacks in Adélies and chinstraps to the ritualized open-bill gape of the gentoo. In fact, incompatibility of agonistic signals may be an important factor in the displacement of gentoos from their breeding colonies by chinstraps. The chinstraps may not be inhibited from attacking by the gentoo's ritualized "air-cushion" (non-contact) threat with open bill. The chinstrap's all-out attack technique, in which feathers are actually plucked, is probably instrumental in dominating the gentoo with its more "sophisticated" behavior. Moreover, gentoo penguins retreat easily, particularly from humans. This general "shyness" has been attributed to contacts with man, and indeed, varies greatly between localities. Gentoos in remote Antarctic rookeries are the most approachable of all gentoos. Since persecution by sealers on many islands of the subantarctic ceased about a century ago, "shyness" does not seem to be a culturally transmitted trait. Rather, it is assumed that it was brought about by inadvertent artificial selection by sealers (Jouventin 1982).

Mutual preening as display seems still correlated with the occurrence of ectoparasites: Antarctic penguins do not preen mutually, and they have practically no ectoparasites. Little blue penguins, on the other extreme, spend much time preening each other, and are heavily infested with mites and other parasites. Moreover, they preen those body regions of the partner that it cannot reach itself (Jouventin 1982).

The color markings of the head are assumed to aid in recognition of conspecifics both at sea (Murphy 1936) and on land (Jouventin 1982). In courtship displays, color markings are "shown" to their best advantage, mostly by males to females. However, sexual selection would have resulted in sexual dimorphism of head markings. Indeed, only initial pair formation depends on recognition of color patterns in rockhopper, macaroni, and king penguins, as birds experimentally deprived of their yellow plumes or orange ear spots, respectively, formed significantly fewer pairs than intact penguins (Jouventin 1982). Later recognition of mates depends on voice rather than on optical signals. Vocal dimorphism between the sexes is most pronounced in species with the least physical dimorphism (Jouventin 1982).

In penguins, olfactory communication appears to be unimportant. In the Adélie penguin, for instance, the olfactory lobe of the brain is of medium size, while petrels have the largest of all birds (Bang 1971).

## LIFE HISTORY STRATEGIES

Penguins in general can be characterized as being K-selected. K-selected species are in balance with their resources, have few young, mature late, take sophisticated care of young, and are less likely to colonize new areas in a short time as "r-selected" species, such as many small rodents, do. The limiting factor for the carrying capacity for most species in the Subantarctic and Antarctic appears to be the available land area that is suitable for breeding, i.e. not only ice-free, but also free of snow cover early in the season when breeding has to commence. Food does not seem to limit penguin numbers, especially since the depletion of whale and seal stocks that competed for the same food (krill, small fish and squid, depending on species), even though the marine food organisms may be patchily distributed, and unpredictable in location and abundance.

Comparisons of age-dependent allocation of energetic priorities, primarily growth, survivorship (including anti-predator behavior), reproduction and intraspecific competition would be a rewarding venture, but, with exception of the Adélie penguin, for most species not enough details are known yet. In the better investigated Adélie and emperor penguins annual mortality is highest among immature birds. Reproductive maturity occurs comparatively late (3–8 years of age in the Adélie; Ainley et al., 1983). Annual mortality of both sexes is equal only in those species where both sexes share equally in incubation. By contrast, male mortality is higher than for females in the emperor penguin (Jouventin 1982).

Clutch size has been assumed to be geared to the ability of the parents to raise a certain number of young per year successfully (Lack 1947, 1948). Although strong selection pressure for clutch size to be kept small may also be expected in rigorous or unpredictable environments (Cody 1966), this expectation is not always satisfied: The largest number of eggs in 1 clutch, 3 or 4, is sometimes found in gentoo penguins (it is not clear, however whether or not these eggs have been laid by more than 1 female), and the Galapagos penguin lays 2–3 clutches per year, totaling 4–6 eggs as an adaptation to an unpredictable environment (Boersma 1976). A typical clutch for most penguin species consists of 2 eggs. In the Antarctic, Adélies, for instance, fledge only about 1 chick from 2 eggs. But the number of successfully reared young varies greatly with the weather conditions in different years. The most specialized penguins, the two *Aptenodytes* species, have reduced the number of eggs laid to 1 and have replaced quantity by quality: they have developed efficient caretaking behavior.

Evolutionary biologists continue to be puzzled by the peculiar trait of the crested penguins to lay 2 eggs of different size. The smaller egg is laid first. The size ratio ranges from 1.71 in the macaroni to 1.17 in the Fjordland crested penguin (Warham 1975). Although the smaller egg is usually viable, at least in the rockhoppers and macaronis (Gwynn 1953a; Downes et al. 1955), it is typically lost from the nest long before the chicks are due to hatch. Warham suggests that crested penguins are able to raise only one chick, and that the first, small egg is insurance against egg loss early when males fight a lot. Thus, the first, small egg is an evolutionary response to "selection favoring aggressive males, selection that is beneficial to the species but detrimental to egg survival" (Warham 1975). Size dimorphism of eggs appears to ensure the raising of only 1 chick. If both hatch, the larger chick will crowd out the smaller one. If only the small egg hatches, the initially small chick will attain the size of a chick from a larger egg within 2 days (Warham 1975). The dual egg size seems to be an ancient trait of the crested penguins, as all species show it, despite their living in a variety of habitats, climates and latitudes. Earlier suggestions that crested penguins are on the way to having only one egg, or that the different egg sizes are the beginning of sex dimorphism, with large eggs producing males, smaller ones females, currently find little support.

A deeper understanding of the evolution of penguins and their behavior must await more detailed studies of functions of behavior and life history strategies of more, preferably all, penguin species. The uneven coverage of the various species is currently a serious obstacle to generalizations. Furthermore, intraspecific variation of ecology and behavior has to be documented more fully as a basis for interspecific comparisons. To this end, the pioneering model studies have to be broadened to investigations of the same species under many different geographical and climatic conditions.

# REFERENCES

Ainley, D.G. 1975. Displays of Adélie penguins: a reinterpretation. In *The Biology of Penguins*, edited by B. Stonehouse, 503–555, MacMillan, London.

Ainley, D.G., and W.B. Emison. 1972. Sexual size dimorphism in Adélie penguins. *Ibis* 114:267–271.

Ainley, D.G., and R.P. Schlatter. 1972. Chick raising ability in Adélie penguins. *Auk* 89:559–566.

Ainley, D.G., R.E. LeResche, and W.J.L. Sladen. 1983. *Breeding Biology of the Adélie Penguin*. Univ. Calif. Press, Berkeley, 240 p.p.

Alexander, W.B., and G. Niethammer. 1959. *Die Vögel der Meere*. Hamburg: Parey, 221 pp.

Ar, A., C.V. Paganelli, B.B. Beeves, D.C. Green, and H. Rahn. 1974. The avian egg: water vapor conductance, shell thickness, and functional pore area. *Condor* 76, 153–158.

Bagshawe, T.W. 1938. Notes on the habits of the Gentoo and Ringed or Antarctic penguins. *Trans. Zool. Soc. London* 24:185–306.

Bang, B.G. 1971. Functional Anatomy of the olfactory system in 23 orders of birds. *Acta Anat. Suppl.* 58: 1–76.

Barkley, R.A. 1968. *Oceanographic Atlas of the Pacific Ocean*. Univ. Hawaii Press, Honolulu.

Boersma, Dee P. 1975. Adaptation of Galapagos penguins for life in two different environments. *The Biology of Penguins*, edited by B. Stonehouse. 101–14. London: Macmillan.

_____. 1976. An ecological and behavioral study of the Galapagos penguin. *Living Bird* 15:43–93.

Boersma, P.D. 1978. Breeding patterns of Galápagos penguins as an indicator of oceanographic conditions. Science *200*, 1481–1483.

Boswall, J. 1972. The South American sea lion *Otaria byronica* as a predator on penguins. *Bull. Brit. Orn. Cl.* 92:129–132.

Boswall, J., and D. MacIver. 1975. The Magellanic penguin *Spheniscus magellanicus*. In *The Biology of Penguins*, edited by B. Stonehouse. 271–305. London: MacMillan.

Boswall, J. and R.J. Prytherch. 1972. Some notes on the birds of Point Tombo, Argentina. *Bull. Brit. Orn. Cl.* 92:118–29.

Brown, K.G. 1957. The leopard seal at Heard Island 1951–54. *Austral. Nat. Antarc. Res. Exp., Interim Rep.* 16:1–34.

Budd, G.M. 1961. The biotopes of emperor penguin rookeries. *Emu* 61:171–189.


_____. 1975. The king penguin *Aptenodytes patagonica* at Heard Island. In *The Biology of Penguins*, edited by B. Stonehouse, 337–62. MacMillan: London.


Burley, N. 1981. Mate choice by multiple criteria in a monogamous species. *Am. Nat.* 117:518–28.

Butler, R.G., and D. Müller-Schwarze. 1977. Penguin census by aerial photographic analysis at Cape Crozier, Ross Island. *Antarct. J. of the U.S.* 12:25–7.


Carcelles, A. 1931. Notas sobre algunas aves de la Isla de Sud Georgia. *Hornero* 4:398–401.

Carrick, R., and S.E. Ingham. 1967. Antarctic seabirds as subjects for ecological research. In *Proceedings of Symposium on Pacific-Antarctic Sciences*, edited by T. Nagata. Tokyo, 1966 Japan. Antarct. Res. Exped. Scient. Rep. Spec. Issue No. 1, 151–84. Dept. Polar Res., Tokyo.

Cendron, J. 1953. La mue du Manchot Adélie adulte. *Alauda* 21:77–84.

Cherry-Gerrard, A. 1922. *The Worst Journey in the World*. London: Chatto and Windus (reprinted 1948 and 1965). 584 pp.

Cody, M. 1966. A general theory of clutch size. *Evolution* 20:174–184.

Conroy, J.W.H., O.H.S. Darling, and H.G. Smith. 1975. The annual cycle of the chinstrap penguin, *Pygoscelis antarctica*, on Signy Island, South Orkney Islands. In *The Biology of Penguins*, edited by B. Stonehouse, 353–362. London: Macmillan.

Conway, W.G. 1965. The penguin metropolis of Punto Tombo. *Animal Kingdom*, 4:115–23.

Crowther, W.E.L.H. 1970. Captain J.W. Robinson's narrative of a sealing voyage to Heard Island, 1858–60. *Polar Record* 15:305–16.

Croxall, J.P. 1982. Energy costs of incubation and molt in petrels and penguins. J. Anim. Ecol. *51*, 177–194.

Croxall, J.P., and E.D. Kirkwood. 1979. *The Distribution of Penguins on the Antarctic Peninsula and Islands of the Scotia Sea*. Cambridge, England: *Brit. Antarctic Survey*, 186 pp.

Croxall, J.P., and P.A. Prince. 1980. The food of Gentoo penguins, *Pygoscelis papua* and Macaroni penguins, Eudyptes chrysolophus, at South Georgia. *Ibis*, 122:245–53.

Davis, L.S. 1982. Timing of nest relief and its effect on breeding success in Adélie penguins. Condor *84*, 178–183.

Derenne, P., P. Jouventin, and J.L. Mougin. 1979. Le chant du Manchot royal (*Aptenodytes patagonicus*) et sa signification évolutive. *Le Gerfaut* 69:211–224.

Despin, B., J.L. Mougin and M. Segonzac. 1972. *Oiseaux et Mammifères de l'Ile de l'Est.* C.N.F.R.A. 31, 106 pp.

Downes, M.C., E.H.M. Ealey, A.M. Gwynn and P.S. Young. 1959. *The Birds of Heard Island.* Austr. Nat. Antarct. Res. Exped. Rep., Ser. B, No. 1, 135 pp.

Eggleton, P. and W.R. Siegfried. 1979. Displays of the jackass penguin. *The Ostrich* 50:139–167.

Eklund, C.R. and F.E. Charlton. 1959. Measuring the temperatures of incubating penguin eggs. *Amer. Sci.* 47:80–86.

Emison, W.B. 1968. Feeding preferences of the Adélie penguin at Cape Crozier, Ross Island. In *Antarctic Bird Studies*, edited by O.L. Austin, 191–212. Antarc. Res. Ser.

Emlen, J.T. and R.L. Penney. 1964. Distance navigation in the Adélie penguin. *Ibis* 106:417–431.

Goldsmith, R. and W.J.L. Sladen. 1961. Temperature regulation of some antarctic penguins. *J. Physiol.* 157:251–62.

Guillottin, M. and Jouventin, P. 1979. La Parade nuptiale du manchot empereur et sa signification biologique. *Biol. Behav. 4*, 249–264.

Gwynn, A.M. 1953a. The egg-laying and incubation periods of rockhopper, macaroni and gentoo penguins. Austral. Nat. Antarc. Res. Exp., Rep. Ser. B, 1, 1–27.

———. 1953b. The status of the leopard seal at Heard Island and Macquarie Island 1948–50. *Austral. Nat. Antarc. Res. Exp., Interim Rep.* 3.

Hui, C.A. 1981. The aerial flight of penguins. Amer. Zool. *21*, 924

Johnson, A.W. 1965. *The birds of Chile and adjacent regions of Argentina, Bolivia, and Peru*, Vol. 1. Buenos Aires: Platt Establecimientos Graficos, S.A.

Jouventin, P. 1975. Mortality parameters in emperor penguins, *Aptenodytes forsteri*. In *The Biology of Penguins*, edited by B. Stonehouse, 435–46. London: MacMillan.

———. 1982. Visual and vocal signals in penguins, their evolution and adaptive characters. *Adv. in Ethology 24*, 149 pp. Berlin: Parey.

Jouventin, P., M. Guillotin, and A. Cornet. 1979. Le chant du Manchot empereur (*Aptenodytes forsteri*) et sa signification adaptive. *Behaviour* 70:231–50.

Kinsky, F.C. 1960. The yearly cycle of the northern blue penguin *Eudyptula minor novaehollandiae*, in the Wellington Harbour area. *Rec. Dom. Mus.* 3:145–218.

Kooyman, G.L. 1975. Behavior and physiology of diving. In *The Biology of Penguins*, edited by B. Stonehouse, 115–37. London: Macmillan.

Kooyman, G.L., C.M. Drabek, R. Eisner, and W.B. Campbell. Diving behavior of the emperor penguin, *Aptenodytes forsteri*. 1971. *Auk* 88:775–795.

Kooyman, G.L., R.W. Davis, J.P. Croxall, and D.P. Costa. 1982. Diving depths and energy requirements of king penguins. *Science* 217:726–727.

Lack, D. 1947/48. The significance of clutch size. *Ibis* 89:302–52; 90: 25–45.

_____. 1966. *Population studies of birds.* Oxford: Clarendon Press, 341 pp.

LeResche, R.W. and W.J.L. Sladen. 1970. Establishment of pair and breeding site bonds by young known-age Adélie penguins (*Pygoscelis adeliae*). *Anim. Behav.* 18:517–526.

Maher, W. 1966. Predation's impact on penguins. *Nat. Hist. N. York* 75 (Jan.):42–50.

Matthews, L.H. 1929. The birds of South Georgia. *Discovery Rep.* 1:561–592.

Modinger, B.A. 1983. A preliminary report on the status and distribution of the Humboldt penguin in Chile. Unpubl. Manuscript.

Mougin, J.L. 1968. Notes sur le cycle reproducteur et la mue du manchot Adélie (*Pygoscelis adeliae*) dans l'Archipel de Pointe Géologie (Terre Adélie). *Oiseau* 38:89–94.

Müller-Schwarze, D. 1968. Circadian rhythms of activity in the Adélie penguin (*Pygoscelis adeliae*) during the austral summer. In *Antarctic Bird Studies*, edited by O.L. Austin, 133–49.

_____. 1978. Play behavior in young Adélie penguins. In *The Evolution of Play Behavior*, edited by D. Müller-Schwarze, 375–77. Benchmark Books in Animal Behavior, Vol. 10. Stroudsburg, Penn. Ross, Dowden, and Hutchinson.

Müller-Schwarze, D. and C. Müller-Schwarze. 1971. Seeleoparden des Ross-Meeres. *Das Tier* 11:38–43.

_____. 1972. Wilson's Stonehut at Cape Crozier. *Antarc. J. U.S.* 7:15–17.

_____. 1973. Differential predation of South Polar skuas in an Adélie penguin rookery. *Condor* 75:127–31.

_____. 1975a. Relations between leopard seals and Adélie penguins. In *The Biology of the Seal*, edited by L.K. Ronald. 394–404. Copenhagen: IUCN. Rapp. Procès-Verbaux Réunions Cons. Intern. Int. Explor. Mer. 169. Charlottenlund Slot, Denmark.

_____. 1975b. A survey of 24 rookeries of pygoscelid penguins in the Antarctic Peninsula area. In *The Biology of Penguins*, edited by B. Stonehouse, 309–20. Macmillan: London.

_____. 1977. Interactions between South Polar skuas and Adélie penguins. In *Adaptations within Antarctic Ecosystems*, edited by G.A. Llano, 619–46. Proc. Third SCAR Symp. Antarct. Biol., Wash., D.C. Smithson. Instit., Wash., D.C.

_____. 1980. Display rate and speed of nest relief in Antarctic pygoscelid penguins. *Auk* 97:825–31.

Müller-Schwarze, D., R. Butler, P. Belanger, M. Bekoff, and A. Bekoff. 1975. Feeding territories of South Polar skuas at Cape Crozier. *Antarct. J. of the U.S.* 10:121–122.

Murphy, R.C. 1936. *Oceanic Birds of South America.* New York, 2 vols.

_____. 1959. History of the penguins. *Nat. Hist. N. York* 68:153–60.

Nice, M.M. 1957. Nesting success in altricial birds. *Auk* 74:305–21.

O'Brien, P.J. 1940. Some observations on the breeding habits and general characteristics of the white-flippered penguin (*Eudyptula albosignata* Finsch). *Rec. Canterbury Mus.* 4(6):311.

Oelke, H. 1975. Breeding behaviour and success in a colony of Adélie penguins *Pygoscelis adeliae*, at Cape Crozier, Antarctica. In *The Biology of Penguins*, edited by B. Stonehouse, 363–395, London: MacMillan.

Penney, R.L. 1964. The Adélie penguin's faithfulness of territory and mate. In *Biologie Antarctique*, edited by R. Carrick, M. Holdgate, and J. Prévost, 401–06. Paris.

_____. 1967. Molt in the Adélie penguin. *Auk* 84:61–71.

_____. 1968. Territorial and social behavior in the Adélie penguin. In *Antarctic Bird Studies*, edited by O.L. Austin, 83–131. Antarc. Res. Ser. 12.

Penney, R.L. and J.T. Emlen. 1967. Further experiments on distance navigation in the Adélie penguin, *Pygoscelis adeliae*. *Ibis* 109:99–109.

Penney, R.L. and G. Lowry. 1967. Leopard seal predation on Adélie penguins. *Ecology* 48:878–82.

Peterson, R.T. 1978. Penguins and their interactions with men. *Intern. Zoo. Yearbook* 18:2–6.

Pettingill, O.S., Jr. 1960. Crèche behavior and individual recognition in a colony of the Rockhopper penguin. *Wilson Bull.* 72:209–221.

Pinshow, B., M.A. Fedak, D.R. Battles, and K. Schmidt-Nielsen. 1976. Energy expenditure for thermoregulation and locomotion in emperor penguins. *Amer. J. Physiol.* 213:903–912.

Pinshow, B., M.A. Fedak, and K. Schmidt-Nielsen. 1977. Terrestrial locomotion in penguins: It costs more to waddle. *Science* 195:592–94.

Prévost, J. 1961. Ecologie du Manchot Empereur. *Exp. Pol. Franç. Publ. Nr. 222.* Paris, 204 pp.

Prévost, J. and F. Bourlière. 1975. Vie sociale et thermoregulation chez le Manchot Empereur. *Alauda* 25(3):167–173.

Rand, R.W. 1960. The biology of guano-producing seabirds. The distribution, abundance and feeding habits of the Cape penguin, *Spheniscus demersus*, off the southwestern coast of Cape Province, *Invest. Rep. Fish S. Afr.* 41:1–28.

Randall, R.M., Randall, B.M., and Beran, J. 1980. Oil pollution and penguins—Is cleaning justified? *Mar. Pollut. Bull.* 11(8):234–37.

Reilly, P.N. and J.M. Cullen. 1979. The little penguin *Eudyptula minor* in Victoria; I: Mortality of adults. *Emu* 79:97–102.

_____. 1981. The little penguin *Eudyptula minor* in Victoria, II: Breeding. *Emu* 81:1–19.

Richdale, L.E. 1940. Random notes on the genus Eudyptula on the Otago Peninsula, New Zealand. *Emu* 40:180–217.

_____. 1941a. A brief summary of the history of the yellow-eyed penguin. *Emu* 40:265–85.

_____. 1941b. The erect-crested penguin (*Eudyptes sclateri* Buller). *Emu* 41:25–53.

_____. 1950. Further notes on the erect-crested penguin. *Emu* 49:153–66.

_____. 1951. *Sexual behavior in penguins*. Lawrence, Kansas: Univ. Kansas Press, 316 pp.

_____. 1957. *A population study of penguins*. Oxford: Clarendon Press, 195 pp.

Risebrough, R.W. and G.M. Carmignani. 1972. Chlorinated hydrocarbons in Antarctic birds. In *Conservation Problems in Antarctica*, edited by B.C. Parker, pp. 63–78, VPI Blacksburg, Virginia.

Roberts, S., and Roberts, B.B. 1940. The breeding behavior of penguins with special reference to *Pygoscelis papua*. *Sci. Rep. Brit. Grahamland Exp. 1934–37.* 1(3):195–254.

Sapin-Jaloustre, J. 1952. Découverte et description de la rookerie d'*Aptenodytes forsteri* de Pointe-Géologie.*L'Oiseau et la Revue française d'Ornithologie* 22:192 and 225–60.

_____. 1960. Écologie du Manchot Adélie. *Exp. Pol. Franç. Publ. Nr. 208.* Paris, 211 pp.

Searcy, W.A. and K. Yasukawa. 1983. Sexual selection and red-winged blackbirds. *Amer. Sci.* 71:166–74.

Selander, R.K. 1972. Sexual selection and dimorphism in birds. In *Sexual Selection and the Descent of Man*, edited by B. Campbell, 180–230. Chicago: Aldine.

Siegfried, W.R., P.G.H. Frost, J.B. Kinahan, and J. Cooper. 1975. Social Behaviour of Jackass penguins at sea. *Zool. Afric. 10*, 87–100.

Simpson, G.G. 1946. Fossil penguins. *Bull. Amer. Mus. Nat. Hist.* 87:9–99.

_____. 1975. Fossil penguins. In *The Biology of Penguins*, edited by B. Stonehouse, 19–41. London: MacMillan, 555 pp.

Sladen, W.J.L. 1955. Some aspects of the behavior of the Adélie and chinstrap penguins. *Acta XI Congr. Intern. Ornithol. Basel*, 241–47.

_____. 1958. The Pygoscelid penguins. 1. Method of study. 2. The Adélie penguin. *Falkl. Isl. Dep. Survey, Sci. Rep.* 17:1–97.

Sladen, W.J.L. 1964. The distribution of the Adélie and chinstrap penguins. In *Antarctic Biology*, edited by R. Carrick, M. Holdgate, and J. Prévost, 359–65. Paris: Hermann.

Sladen, W.J.L., C.M. Menzie, and W.L. Reichel. 1966. DDT residues in Adélie penguins and a crabeater seal from Antarctica: Ecological implications. *Nature 210*: 670–673.

Sladen, W.J.L., J.C. Boyd, and J.M. Pedersen. 1966. Biotelemetry studies on penguin body temperature. *Antarc. J. U.S.* 1:142–43.

Sparks, J. and T. Soper. 1967. *Penguins*. New York: Taplinger, 263 pp.

Spurr, E.B. 1977. Adaptive significance of the reoccupation period of the Adélie penguin. In *Adaptations within Antarctic Ecosystems*, edited by G.A. Llano, 605–18. *Proc. 3rd SCAR Symp. Antarctic Biology.* Wash., D.C.: Smithsonian Inst., 1252 pp.

Stevenson, M.R., O. Guillen, and Santoro de Ycaza, J. 1970. *Marine Atlas of the Pacific Coastal Waters of South America*. Univ. Calif. Press, Berkeley and Los Angeles.

Stonehouse, B. 1952. Breeding Behaviour of the Emperor Penguin. *Nature* 169:760.

_____. 1953. The Emperor Penguin *Aptenodytes forsteri* Gray. 1. Breeding behaviour and development. *Falkl. Isl. Dep. Survey, Sci. Rep.* 6, 33 pp.

_____. 1960. The King penguin *Aptenodytes patagonica* of South Georgia. 1. Breeding behaviour and development. *Falkl. Isl. Dep. Survey, Sci. Rep.* 23, 81 pp.

_____. 1968. *Penguins. The World of Animals Series* London: Barker and New York: Golden Press, 96 pp.

_____. 1971. The Snares crested penguin. *Ibis* 113:1–7.

Strange, I.J. 1965. Beauchene Island. *Polar Rec.* 12:725–30.

_____. 1981. *The Falkland Islands.* Newton Abbot and London: David and Charles, 256 pp.

Taylor, R.H. 1962. The Adélie penguin, *Pygoscelis adeliae* at Cape Royds. *Ibis* 104:176–204.

Thomson, R.B. 1977. Effects of human disturbance on an Adélie penguin rookery and measures of control. In *Adaptations within Antarctic Ecosystems*, 1177–80, *Proceed. 3rd SCAR Symp. Antarct. Biol.* Washington, D.C.: Smithsonian Institution.

Todd, F.S. 1980. Factors influencing emperor penguin mortality at Cape Crozier and Beaufort Island, Antarctica. *Le Gerfaut* 70:37–49.

Trillmich, F. 1978. Feeding territories and breeding success of South Polar skuas. *Auk.* 95:23–33.

Trivelpiece, W. 1981. Ecological studies of pygoscelid penguins and Antarctic skuas. Ph.D. Diss. S.U.N.Y. Coll. Envir. Sci. Forestry, Syracuse, N.Y. 136 pp.

Trivelpiece, W. and N.J. Volkman. 1979. Nest site competition between Adélie and chinstrap penguins: an ecological interpretation. *Auk* 96:675–81.

Volkman, N.J., P. Presler, and W. Trivelpiece. 1980. Diets of pygoscelid penguins at King George Island, Antarctica. *Condor* 82:373–78.

Warham, J. 1958. The nesting of the little penguin (*Eudyptula minor*) *Ibis* 100:605–616.

_____. 1963. The rockhopper penguin, *Eudyptes chrysocome*, at Macquarie Island. *Auk* 80:229–56.

_____. 1971. Aspects of breeding behaviour in the Royal penguin, *Eudyptes chrysolophus schlegeli. Notornis* 18:91–115.

_____. 1972a. Breeding seasons and sexual dimorphism in rockhopper penguins. *Auk* 89:86–105.

_____. 1972b. Aspects of the biology of the erect-crested penguin, *Eudyptes sclateri. Ardea* 60:145–84.

_____. 1974a. The Fjordland crested penguin. *Ibis* 116:1–27.

_____. 1974b. The breeding biology and behaviour of the Snares crested penguin. J. Roy. Soc. N.Z. 4, 63–108.

_____. 1975. The crested penguins. In *The Biology of Penguins*, edited by B. Stonehouse, 189–269. London: Macmillan, 555 pp.

Watson, G.E., J.P. Angle, P.C. Harper, M.A. Bridge, R.P. Schlatter, W.L.N. Tickell, J.C. Boyd, and M.M. Boyd. 1971. *Birds of the Antarctic and Subantarctic.* Antarctic Map Folio Series, Fol. 14, Amer. Geogr. Soc.

Williams, A.J. 1980. Aspects of the breeding biology of the gentoo penguin, *Pygoscelis papua. Gerfaut* 70(3):283–95.

Wood, R.C. 1971. Population dynamics of breeding South Polar skuas of unknown age. *Auk* 88:805–14.

Yeates, G.W. 1968. Studies on the Adélie penguin at Cape Royds 1964–65 and 1965–66. *New Zealand J. Marine Res.* 2:472–96.

_____. 1971. Diurnal activity in the Adélie penguin (*Pygoscelis adeliae*) at Cape Royds, Antarctica. *J. Nat. Hist.* 5:103–12.

Young, E. 1963. Feeding habits of the South Polar skua *Catharacta maccormicki.* *Ibis* 105:301–17.

Zinderen Bakker, E.M. van, Jr. 1971. A behaviour analysis of the gentoo penguin. In *Marion and Prince Edward Islands*, edited by E.M. van Zinderen Bakker Jr., J.M. Winterbottom, and R.A. Dyer, 251–72. Capetown: A.A. Balkema, 427 pp.

# INDEX

Please note that the entries are by specific behaviors, places, etc., instead of by species, as the species can be easily found under their respective chapter headings. Thus, the breeding age of the emperor penguin will be found under "Breeding age, Emperor penguin", rather than under "Emperor penguin".

598.441  Muller-Schwarze,
MUL        Dietland.

       The behavior of
       penguins

| DATE | | |
|---|---|---|
| | | |
| | | |
| | | |
| | | |
| | | |
| | | |
| | | |
| | | |
| | | |
| | | |
| | | |
| | | |
| | | |

29.50

© THE BAKER & TAYLOR CO.